Comprehensive Security for Data Centers and Mission Critical Facilities

(Including EMP Protection)

Luis Ayala

ISBN-13: 978-1987617597

PREFACE

This book was written primarily for the Data Center industry. These books consist of a general discussion of risk assessments and security threats to mission critical facilities and much of the information is applicable to many building types so they are widely available. The book was purposely written as a high-level discussion with little detail for obvious security reasons.

A Supplement to this book will be "crowd-sourced" describing specific threats and includes practical applications and recommendations for mitigating those threats. Crowd-sourcing by asking data center operators to contribute specific examples of threats they've encountered and how they dealt with those threats is used for several reasons. First of all, no one knows more about threats to data centers and practical solutions than the data center operators. Secondly, no one data center operator has seen it all. Sharing threat information across the industry will allow data center operators to evaluate their facilities and operations with the benefit of the cumulative experiences of other data center operators.

Recent developments in the field of EMP prompted me to include the subject in this book. Here is a quote from the Chinese book, "The Science of Military Strategy" published in 2013 by China's Military Strategic Research Department, Academy of Military Science.

领域的竞争更加激烈，电磁、激光等新概念武器不久就可投入实战使

用，量子技术、生物计算机技术的突破可能引起新的军事革命

This roughly translates to (please excuse my translation as only a Chinese language version of the book is available):

"Competition in the field has become more intense, and new concept weapons such as *electromagnetic* and laser will soon be put into action. Use, breakthrough in quantum technology, biological computer technology may lead to new military revolution…."

Because of the sensitivity of the subject, distribution of the Supplement will be tightly controlled.

Luis Ayala
Louayala16@gmail.com

Table of Contents

1. OVERVIEW

What are Mission Critical facilities? Mission Critical facilities must operate 8,760 hours per year without interruption. Because of my background in the Department of Defense (DoD), naturally I tend to think of mission critical facilities as those required by the military in support of the warfighter. Although most data centers are operated for commercial customers, increasingly the Department of Defense is beginning to contract for data center service from commercial suppliers and in many cases, DoD requires that the data center comply with Department of defense security requirements. That said, I will endeavor to include the requirements DoD expects so that your data center can meet those requirements should the need arise.

First-order examples that quickly come to mind include hospitals, data centers, power plants, electrical distribution, natural gas pipelines, refineries, water treatment plants, sewage treatment plants, telecommunications facilities, and military installations. This is by no means a complete list and this book focuses on a generic facility consisting of an existing building with a technical workforce to cover the hazards and possible defenses and protection strategies. Supplements to this generic document are under development with information specific to that type such as hospitals, data centers, etc.

Of course, first-order mission critical facilities rely on a host of second- and third-order facilities that are critical for efficient day-to-day operation. Examples of second order support facilities include commercial utilities leading to the site, roads, airports, police and fire fighters, hospitals and educational institutions. In order to ensure high availability, mission critical facilities install redundant systems capable of taking over in the event of disruption to primary systems. But, how much attention is paid to the service providers that support mission critical facilities? Are vendors and suppliers that frequent the facility properly trained, vetted and monitored for suspicious behavior?

Risk Assessment

Defense of any facility begins with a well-documented risk assessment. At a very basic level, the owner's level of acceptable risk includes factors such as life safety, property protection, economic loss, regulatory impact, and redundant offsite processing. An effective risk assessment also takes into account human variables such as workforce capability (adequate training and career development), stability (competitive pay and benefits, advancement opportunity) and behavioral monitoring (family/work life balance).

Hazards

The International Building Code (IBC) defines a "electronic data processing" building under "Group B Business Occupancies" and sets a basic set of minimum requirements to safeguard the general health and welfare of occupants such as structural, sanitation, lighting, ventilation, and life safety. NFPA 101: Life Safety Code, has a more detailed perspective regarding occupancy-type classification than IBC and is limited to life safety. NFPA does not define an "electronic data processing" facility so it is debatable as to what a data center is per NFPA 101 based on the occupancy patterns and characteristic hazards in a data center environment. I assume that if NFPA 101 defines a modern telephone exchange as an industrial occupancy, that classification should also apply to data centers.

Why is this important? NFPA 101 lists a "special purpose" industrial-occupancy subset that is described as an industrial occupancy in which ordinary and low-hazard industrial operations are conducted and characterized by a relatively low density of employee population, with much of the area occupied by machinery or equipment. The special-purpose industrial-occupancy subset does allow a significant reduction in the egress requirements for a facility. That has direct relationship with the physical security of a data center.

For many years, NFPA 75 has been the standard of care for fire protection of IT equipment. DoD, GSA and VA design manuals and standards require the provisions of NFPA 75 be adhered to in full, with certain additional provisions. Compliance with NFPA 75 is rarely required by local building or fire codes but is routinely applied to IT equipment facilities on a prescriptive basis. A documented risk assessment is the basis for implementation of the standard for commercial facilities.

Previously, NFPA 75-2013 contained statements that run counter to the 24x7 requirement for data centers such as Section 8.4.2.1, which stated "the power to all electronic equipment shall be disconnected upon activation of a gaseous-agent total flooding system..." The NFPA 75-2017 edition made significant changes to the minimum level of requirements to protect IT equipment from fire and the effects of fire.

Energy Efficiency

ASHRAE 90.4-2016: Energy Standard for Data Centers is the stand-alone standard applicable to data centers for building envelope, service-water heating, lighting, and other requirements. It introduced new terminology for demonstrating compliance including the design and annual mechanical load component (MLC) and electrical-loss components (ELC). ASHRAE 90.4 also contains references to ASHRAE 90.1. The use of ASHRAE 90.1 is compulsory to demonstrate minimum energy conformance for commercial buildings (including data centers) in many jurisdictions. ASHRAE 90.1-2010 edition introduced in-depth requirements for computer rooms and added a new term, "sensible coefficient of performance" (SCOP), the energy use benchmark for computer and data processing room (CDPR) air conditioning units.[1] SCOP divides the net sensible cooling capacity (in watts) by the input power (in watts).

---

[1] The definition of SCOP and the detail on how the units are to be tested comes from the Air Conditioning, Heating, and Refrigeration Institute (AHRI) in conjunction with the American National Standards Institute (ANSI) and was published in AHRI/ANSI Standard 1360: Performance Rating of Computer and Data Processing Room Air Conditioners.

2. SITE SECURITY

This section refers to the "Defensive Design" of the actual site which is typically several acres. I use Department of Defense examples because they are comprehensive and they have a couple hundred years' experience preventing unauthorized access by evil-doers. In addition to fences, natural formations such as bodies of water, rough terrain, or densely wooded areas may act as a barrier to define and protect the data center's site perimeter. The primary design strategy is to keep non-employees as far away from the data center as possible. The easiest and least costly opportunity for achieving the appropriate levels of protection is to incorporate sufficient standoff distance into project designs. While sufficient standoff distance is not always available to provide the standoff distances required for conventional construction, maximizing the available standoff distance always results in the most cost-effective solution except where land is at a premium. Maximizing standoff distance also ensures that there are opportunities in the future to expand the building or upgrade to meet increased threats or to accommodate higher levels of protection. If possible, I recommend the data center should be sited at least 300 feet from the campus perimeter.

Access Control Points

The Department of Defense term for site access points is Entry Control Facilities (ECF) and the criteria can be found in UFC- 4-022-01. ECFs are classified according to their intended use as shown below. I will focus the discussion on primary and secondary ECFs.

Use Classification	Operational Hours	FPCON Considerations	Preferred Operation
Primary	24/7 Open continuously	Open thru FPCON Delta	Vehicle registration/visitor pass capacity. Regular operations, visitors with authorization. Could also be designated as truck and delivery gate.
Secondary	Regular hours, closed at times	Potentially closed at or above FPCON Charlie	Regular operations, visitors with authorization. Could also be designated as truck and delivery gate.
Limited Use	Only opened for special purposes	Closed at most times	Tactical vehicles, HAZMAT, special events, etc.
Pedestrian Access	Varies	Potentially closed at or above FPCON Charlie	Personnel only. Could be located near installation housing areas, near schools, or as part of a Primary or Secondary ECF.

An ECF is subdivided into four zones, each encompassing specific functions and operations. Beginning at the installation property boundary, the zones include the approach zone, access control zone, response zone, and the safety zone. Specific components are used within each zone to conduct the necessary operations.

The location of each zone of the ECF is illustrated here.

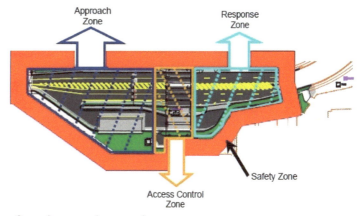

The **Approach Zone** lies between the installation boundary and the Access Control Zone. It is the interface between the off-facility road network and the facility, and the area all vehicles must traverse before reaching the actual checkpoint. The Approach Zone should include design elements to support the following functions and operations:

- Reduce the speed of incoming vehicles to, or below, the design speed of the ECF;
- Perform sorting of traffic by vehicle type, e.g. sorting trucks or visitors into the proper lane before reaching the inspection area or checkpoint;
- Provide adequate stacking distance for vehicles waiting for entry, especially during times of peak demand, to ensure minimal impact on traffic approaching the installation and on traffic safety operations of adjacent public highways; and
- Provide the first opportunity to identify potential threat vehicles, including those attempting entry through the outbound lanes of traffic.

Roadway layout and traffic control devices such as signs, variable message systems, signals, and lane control markings should be utilized to perform these functions. Drivers should be notified of the upcoming access control point, the proper speed to travel, and proper lane to utilize.

The **Access Control Zone** is the main body of the ECF and includes guard facilities and traffic management equipment used by the security forces. The design of the Access Control Zone should be flexible enough to ensure the infrastructure can support future inspection demands, access control equipment, and technologies. Inspection and control of vehicle entry occurs here. The frequency of complete inspections is dependent on the access level of the vehicle owner, but occasional unscheduled vehicles inspections of employee personally operated vehicles (POV) are recommended for ALL individuals. Security personnel should monitor and control both inbound and outbound traffic. If a vehicle is denied entry during identification checks, the access control zone must have room for that vehicle to be re-directed to exit the campus. Traffic arms can be used to control traffic when a vehicle is being rejected from the ECF.

In order to maintain security and barrier safety functions, provide an uninterruptible power supply (UPS) for the Gatehouse and security devices. As a minimum, provide UPS for the following: Primary communications system, duress alarm system, computers, CCTV systems, Intrusion Detection Systems (IDS), Enunciator, and Access Control Equipment including active vehicle barrier controls, barrier activation device (for emergency close), any traffic arms used for safety at the active vehicle barrier, traffic sensors, and barrier signals and warning lights. An

4

IDS consists of interior and exterior sensors, surveillance devices, and associated communication subsystems that collectively detect an intrusion of a specified site, facility or perimeter and annunciate an alarm. The ECF should have a toilet.

The **Response Zone** is the area extending from the end of the Access Control Zone to the final denial barrier. This zone defines the end of the ECF. Provide final denial barriers at the termination of the ECF to provide the capability to stop threat vehicles from using high-speed attacks to gain entry to the installation. The necessary length of the response zone and location of the final denial barriers is based on the provision of adequate response time. The Response Zone should be designed so that the security force has time to react to a threat, operate the final denial barriers, and close the ECF if necessary. Roadway containment is necessary to prevent inbound vehicles from unauthorized access and must extend from the installation perimeter to the final denial barrier in order to be effective. Passive vehicle barriers should encompass a contiguous perimeter around the ECF, with the final denial barriers completing the containment. The barriers should be arranged to ensure that a vehicle couldn't circumvent the ECF once the vehicle has entered.

Determine the acceptable standoff distance or **Safety Zone** by the expected threat. While most data centers don't consider terrorist threats as very likely, the threat posed by criminals is much more likely. Depending on where the data center is located, I recommend a minimum distance of 20 feet as an exclusion zone, 50 feet would be better.

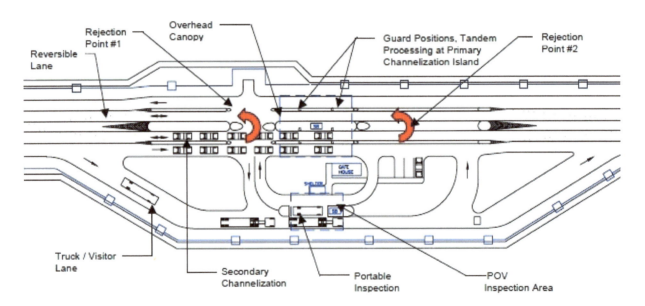

Traffic Control and Parking

Traffic calming, or speed management, should be utilized once a vehicle is on campus to restrict high-speed travel as discussed below:

- Road alignment (circle, serpentine) (ensure that any curves are adequate to support the design vehicles, recommend minimum of AASHTO WB-50 (WB-15m));

- Drop-in or retractable bollards (to cause serpentine traffic flow);
- Gates or barriers that redirect traffic (may be moveable manually or mechanically if not in use);
- Speed humps or speed tables; and
- Pavement texture.

It is also desirable to manage the speed of traffic in inbound and outbound lanes of the ECF for safety. Clearly post the campus speed limit (25 MPH) at the ECF so a driver is made aware on arrival. Speed humps and guard rails should also be used to slow traffic and prevent vehicles from leaving the roadway. Directional traffic spike controllers (back up spikes, spike strips, tire killers, tire rippers, tire shredders, motorized traffic spikes, directional traffic control spikes, spike barriers, etc.) should be installed as needed to prevent entry of unauthorized vehicles.

Vehicle parking on campus should not be allowed closer than 66 feet (20 meters) from the data center. Trash containers typically located on a parking area should not be closer than 13 feet (4 meters) from the data center. Fuel tanks may be located within unobstructed spaces if they do not provide opportunities for concealment of explosives. Standoff distances from the data center for fuel tanks are based on flammability (not explosive equivalence); therefore, they should be determined using NFPA 30.

Site Surveillance

The ECF Gatehouse should meet the minimum ballistic requirements of UL 752 Level V. Many DoD installations desire additional position called an "overwatch" for security personnel to facilitate a response to a threat. These positions are normally placed in the response zone to facilitate surveillance and armed response. This position may be fixed or temporary/portable. Of course, use of security cameras is recommended so security personnel inside the Security Operations Center (SOC) are aware of suspicious activity at the ECF. I highly recommend use Intrusion Detection Systems (IDS) in addition to CCTV. A good IDS will provide an extra set of eyes on the campus fence line and alert security personnel to activity that may be hidden from CCTV. The ECF should have at least two means of communication from the ECF to the SOC, e.g. telephone, data or radio. Coordinate the requirements for radio-based communication with local police. Some data centers may require an emergency ring down telephone, which provides a direct, hard-wired duress alarm to the SOC.

Weather Resistance

Providing an overhead canopy at the access control area can improve lighting, protect the guards and drivers from inclement weather, and serve as a platform for traffic control devices, signage, and security equipment. An overhead canopy should be provided for all posts routinely occupied by security personnel and the inspection lanes unless directed by the installation not to provide the canopy over a portion or all of the posts. The minimum clear height should be 17 ft (5.2 m) to support common vehicle heights and facilitate use of the overhead canopy for lighting or security equipment. The clear height is measured from the pavement to the lowest point on the overhead canopy including light fixtures and other equipment. It would be prudent to install any

HVAC equipment on the roof of the gatehouse to reduce unauthorized access and limit the number of penetrations in the walls.

Perimeter Fence

The physical security barrier provided by a security fence provides the following functions:
- Gives notice of legal boundary of the outermost limits of the protected area.
- Assists in controlling and screening authorized entries into secured/protected areas by channeling vehicles and personnel to access control points.
- Supports surveillance, detection, assessment, and other security functions by providing a platform for installing intrusion detection equipment.
- Deters casual intruders from penetrating a secured/protected area by presenting a barrier that requires an overt action to enter.
- Causes a delay to obtain access to a facility, thereby increasing the probability of detection.

Ornamental Fences

Ornamental (also known as tubular) fencing provides a greater resistance to climbing as well as providing aesthetic qualities in comparison to chain link fencing. Ornamental fencing systems are constructed of either steel or aluminum components. Install the ornamental fence pickets plumb and provide a minimum of 2 inches (51 mm) or maximum of 6 inches (152 mm) between the fence and the ground.

Chain Link Fencing

Chain Link Fencing fabric must be minimum 9-gage wire mesh and mesh openings must not be greater than 2-inches (51 mm) per side. The fencing fabric must be extended to within 2 inches (51 mm) of firm ground and anchored, if required by service requirements, using horizontal bottom rails, tension wires, concrete curbs, sills, sheet piling, piping, or other inexpensive materials. For additional security burying the fabric 12 inches (305 mm) may also be considered; however, corrosion of the buried fabric must be monitored. This anchoring will prevent the fencing fabric from being able to be lifted by hand more than 5 inches (125 mm) in height. Horizontal bottom rails, concrete curbs, or sills can assist in mitigating an intruder from lifting the fence fabric beyond the requirement above. Mesh openings in chain link fencing should not be covered, blocked, or laced with material which would prevent a clear view of personnel, vehicles, or material in outer clear zones. Locate all posts, rails, bracing and tension wires on the secure/protected side, i.e. inner side, of the fencing fabric.

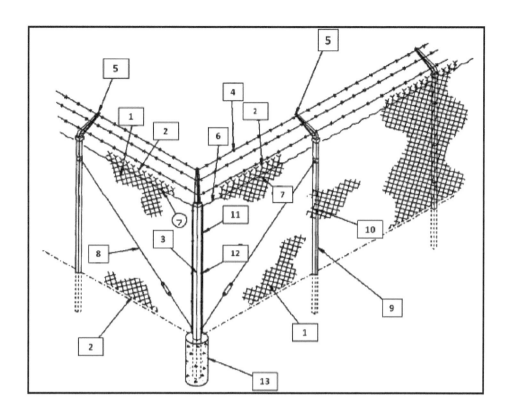

1	Fabric
2	Selvage
3	Corner Post
4	Barbed Wire/Barbed Tape
5	Outrigger/Barbed Wire Arm
6	Tension Wire (Top and Bottom)
7	Hog Ring
8	Truss Rod
9	Line Post
10	Tie Wire
11	Tension Bar
12	Tension Clip
13	Concrete Footing

Welded Wire Mesh Fabric Fencing

Welded wire mesh fabric fencing material is composed of a series of longitudinal and transverse steel wires arranged substantially at right angles to each other and welded together. In comparison to chain link fencing has a greater deterrence to intrusion by climbing and cutting. Welded wire mesh fabric fence openings are relatively small to prevent toe or finger hold. Although the mesh sizes are small, visibility through the fence may be higher than chain link fencing even at slight angles near parallel to the fence line. See ASTM F2453/F2453M for material requirements. Maximum vertical/horizontal opening dimension must be 2 inches (51 mm). Minimum thickness – 9 gage (3.76 mm). Welded wire mesh fabric fencing construction costs in non-urban environments may be approximately one half of ornamental security grade fencing.

Expanded metal fencing can be applied as a retrofit to existing chain link fencing and gates to provide additional protection, strength, and durability. Expanded metal fencing should be installed directly to the existing fence utilizing the installed chain link fence fabric and framework.

Barbed Wire and Barbed Tape Concertina

Barbed wire is a fabricated wire product consisting of two-line wires twisted to form a two-wire strand, into which 2–point or 4–point barbs are tightly wrapped and locked into place at specific intervals. Barbed tape concertina is a strip of metal, machined to produce clusters of sharp points. Provide three strands of barbed wire, equally spaced, on outrigger/support arms where barbed tape/concertina is mounted.

Double Fence Lines

Assets that require Electronic Security Systems (ESS) for perimeter security may require a double fence line. Perimeter ESS and double fence lines typically associated with assets that require a high level of protection for the force or covert entry tactic. This system is intended to increase the probability of detection, decrease nuisance alarms, and prevent access to ESS. The typical configuration is outer clear zone, outer fence, isolation zone, inner fence, and inner clear zone. No sensors should be placed on the outer fence of a double fence line system.

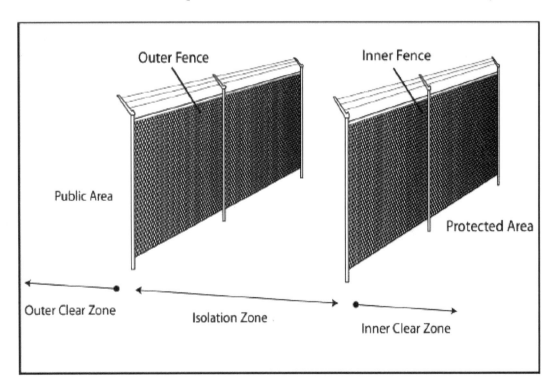

Fence Line Electronic Security Systems

Electronic Security Systems (ESS) may be used to increase the probability of detection and the assessment of intruders attempting to enter restricted areas. ESS includes Intrusion Detection Systems (IDS), Access Control Systems (ACS), and Closed Circuit Television (CCTV) for assessment of alarm conditions. The design of fences and gates must support the site-specific design of the ESS as required.

Drainage Culverts and Utility Openings

Provide protective measures for culverts, storm drains, sewers, air intakes, exhaust tunnels, and utility openings, that have a cross-section area of 96 square inches (61,939 square mm) or greater, with the smallest dimension being more than 6 inches (152.4 mm) and:
- Pass through clear zones.
- Traverse under or through security fences.

Such openings and barrier penetrations must be protected by securely fastened grills, locked manhole covers, or equivalent means to prevent entry or provide forced entry penetration resistance equal that of the fence. Regarding material selection for securing openings and penetrations. If drainage conditions require large diameter pipes, or if it is a more economical approach to provide security protection, drainage openings may be constructed of multiple pipes having individual diameters of 10 inches (250 mm) or less extend multiple pipes through the entire conduit, secured to each other and to the large opening. As an economical alternative, reduce the pipe lengths to short segments approximately 6-inches (152 mm) long. Place the short segments at the attack side of the opening and secure them to the welded bar grill.

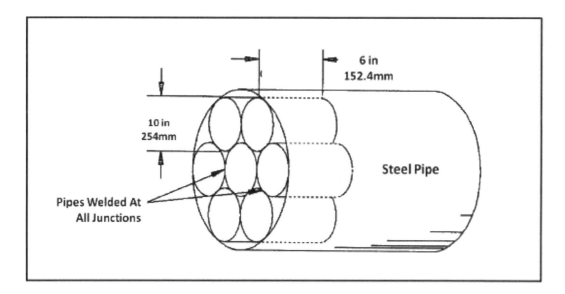

Tunneling Prevention

The soil under the fence must provide a minimum of 15 seconds of tunneling resistance using hand tools. Tunneling prevention must be used in areas containing "soft" soils. "Very soft" and "soft" soils are those that can be extruded between fingers when squeezed and/or molded by light finger pressure. Areas with a soil analysis indicating that "soft" soils are present must embed fencing in a continuous concrete curb. The recommended depth of the curb will be determined from the soil analysis and the frost depth at the facility. The frost depth for the subject areas must be considered to assure that heaving of posts and curb cannot occur during the winter. If the soil analysis does not indicate tunneling may occur quickly, continuous concrete curbing may still be considered as an added protective measure.

Vehicular Gates

Vehicular gates should limit opening sizes when possible to decrease open/close cycle time. There is no maximum height for vehicular gates. Coordinate gate height with the adjacent security fencing and the width will be at least as wide as the road entering the gate. Cantilevered, sliding or wheel supported gates are considered the best selection for vehicle security gates followed by overhead sliding gates, swing gates, vertical tilt and overhead "guillotine" gates. Areas where snow and ice are prevalent may consider using cantilever or swing gates instead of tracked sliding gates. However, if sliding gates are used, consideration should be given to adding internal heating for gate mechanisms. In areas where real estate is tight, vertical tilt gates are recommended.

Drainage Crossing

Fencing passing over ditches or swales is needed to provide protection to prevent unauthorized entry. Ditches and swales that do not receive frequent water flow must provide additional fencing below, suspending from the lower rail of the main fence to the auxiliary frame and around the sides of the ditch. The added fence must be attached every 2 inches (51 mm) along the intersection of the two fence sections and either attached to a series of ground stakes secured to the sides and bottom of the ditch or embedded in a concrete sill in the ditch or swale. Concrete curbing must be used to fill areas between fencing and ground surface.

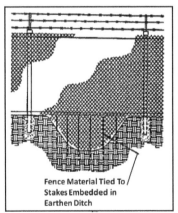
Fence Material Tied To Stakes Embedded in Earthen Ditch

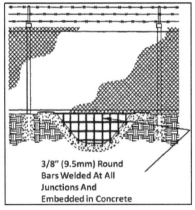
3/8" (9.5mm) Round Bars Welded At All Junctions And Embedded in Concrete

3. BUILDING SECURITY

Buildings designed to protect against direct fire are probably some of the strongest facilities you will find. This document provides guidance for design of new buildings and for retrofits of existing buildings against the effects of direct fire weapons. Attacks against facilities and other assets using direct fire weapons have always been a threat to U.S. Government operations. A direct fire attack requires an unobstructed line-of-sight to the asset being attacked within the effective range of the weapon being used. Aggressors often fire these weapons from vantage points outside the controlled perimeter of an installation or facility, which makes these threats difficult to prevent or to detect before they occur. The aggressors' goals are to damage the facility, to injure or kill its occupants, or to damage or destroy assets. The system of countermeasures that is provided to mitigate the effects of any tactic is referred to as the **protective system**.

Building Construction

Let's start with solid exterior wall construction. Some of these walls can stop a tank round.

Material	Total Wall Thickness [1]
4 inch (100 mm) brick / 2 inch (50 mm) air gap / 8 inch (200 mm) hollow CMU	14 inches (356 mm)
8 inch (200 mm) grout filled CMU	8 inches (200 mm)
8 inch (200 mm) solid brick	8 inches (200 mm)
4 inch (100 mm) brick / 2 inch (50 mm) air gap / 4 inch (100 mm) brick	10 inches (254 mm)
4 inch (100 mm) brick / 4 inch (100 mm) air gap / 4 inch (100 mm) brick	11.5 inches (292 mm)
6 inch (150 mm) reinforced concrete	6 inch (150 mm)
8 inch (200 mm) reinforced concrete	8 inch (200 mm)
12 inch (300 mm) reinforced concrete	12 inch (300 mm)

1. Nominal thicknesses.

Not that you need to worry about tank rounds, but this will give you an idea what I mean by a solid exterior wall. A data center is more likely to be hit by a tornado, an aircraft or a hurricane. The 12-inch concrete is the highest level of protection you're likely gonna need. Of course, you could add steel plate to the inner side to resist EMP, but that's probably overkill. More about that later.

Windows and Doors

The design strategy for a very high level of protection for a data center is the elimination of exterior windows and doors. If windows are installed, laminated glass is preferred as the protective layer (the inner lite in an insulating glass window) in glass windows because when laminated glass fails the laminate interlayer tends to retain the glass fragments, significantly reducing the hazardous fragments entering inhabited areas. Monolithic glass and acrylic should not be allowed because those glazing's break into hazardous fragments. Polycarbonate or other glazing systems may be allowed because they limit fragment hazards. Glazing frame bite requirements for structurally or non-structurally glazed windows or skylights shall be in accordance with ASTM F2248. Apply structural silicone bead or glazing tape to both sides of the glass panel for single pane glazing but only to the inboard side for insulating glass units.

Of course, we have to install fire exits at the building exterior, but the area just inside the doorway should have a corridor with a ninety-degree bend (the bend also helps protect against EMP). Conventional doors should open outwards because in a blast situation, doors tend to rebound off the door frames and fail outwards, resulting in minimal hazards. Doors should also be oriented such that they do not face the campus perimeters or uncontrolled vantage points to minimize vulnerabilities to people entering or leaving buildings. Changing entrance orientation in existing buildings may require significant changes in building operations, such as using an alternate entrance as a main entrance. The option of blocking sight lines is often the most practical for existing buildings. Provide unglazed exterior doors that are tested to achieve a high level of protection in accordance with ASTM F2247 or with ASTM F2927.

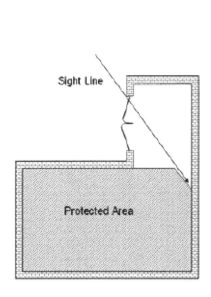
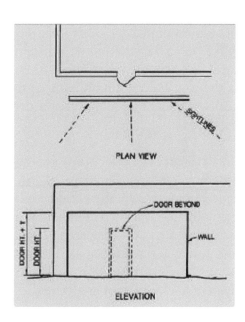

Where there are potential sight lines to assets through vents or other building openings they should be protected similarly to windows and doors. Where shielding walls are used, ensure that their location and configuration are communicated to the mechanical engineers to ensure that their heating, ventilation, and air conditioning designs take the potential for reduced air flow into account.

Roof

Designing a roof to prevent water infiltration is easy. Designing roofs to protect against flying debris from a tornado or to resist direct fire weapons is not so easy. Direct fire (from a rifle) is only an issue where there are sightlines to roofs. I recommend use of high parapets that block sightlines to the roof. Where that is the case, design the roof similar to walls. A high level of protection depends on using materials such as reinforced concrete or steel to provide the necessary resistance. The preferred location for mechanical equipment that takes in outside air for ventilation such as air-conditioners, is on the roof.

Building Layout

For new buildings, ensure that the main entrance to the building does not face a controlled perimeter or other uncontrolled vantage points with direct lines of sight to the entrance or the layout should provide means to block the lines of sight. For existing buildings where the main entrance faces a controlled perimeter, either use a different entrance as the main entrance or screen that entrance to limit the ability of potential aggressors wishing to target people entering and leaving the building. Where main building entrances have sightlines from multiple vantage points at or outside of controlled perimeters, where there are no controlled perimeters, or where it is otherwise infeasible to avoid building entrances facing those vantage points, provide screening or otherwise block lines of sight.

Exterior doors should be positioned such that they will not be propelled into inhabited areas if they fail in response to a blast or provide other means to ensure they are intercepted by a surface with sufficient strength to keep the doors from translating into inhabited areas if they fail or otherwise ensure they do not become hazards to building occupants. To limit opportunities for aggressors placing explosives underneath buildings, ensure that access to crawl spaces, utility tunnels, and other means of under building access is controlled in all buildings required to comply with these standards.

To minimize exposure to direct blast effects and potential impacts from hazardous glass fragments and other potential debris, critical assets and mission-critical equipment or high-risk personnel should be located away from the building exterior. Circulation within buildings should be designed to facilitate visual detection and monitoring of unauthorized personnel approaching controlled areas or occupied spaces. Controlling visitor access maximizes the possibility of detecting potential threatening activities. Locations in buildings where visitor access is controlled should be kept away from sensitive or critical areas, areas where high-risk or mission-critical equipment and personnel are located.

In rooms adjacent to the exterior of the building, personnel and critical equipment should be positioned to minimize exposure to direct blast effects and potential impacts from hazardous glass fragments and other potential debris. Because doors can become hazardous debris during explosive blast events and designing them to resist blast effects is expensive, avoid building configurations that have large numbers of exterior doors leading into inhabited areas. Internal hallways with interior entrances to rooms or suites are preferable.

Acoustics

Yes, sound really can disrupt a hard drive (or an entire data center). Design for acoustics should be done very carefully, in order to coordinate with the architecture, mechanical and structural design. A comprehensive acoustical design must include considerations for sound isolation, building mechanical system noise and vibration control, and room finishes. There are basically two types of sound transmission; airborne and structure-borne. Airborne sound is transmitted through the air (i.e., music).

According to an article that appeared on Gozmodo, a Nasdaq Nordic stock exchange data center in Finland was taken down by its fire suppression system. Similar incidents occurred last year at a Microsoft's Azure data center in Europe and an ING Bank center in Romania in 2016. "When those systems go off there's a shockwave that can disrupt the technology," Greg Schulz, founder of technology advisory and consulting firm StorageIO. Apparently, the release of the gas can come with a shockwave. According to a recent study, Siemens found that vibrations from sound as loud as 110 decibels could damage a hard drive. The fire extinguisher nozzles could be as loud as 130 decibels.

Structure-borne sound is transmitted through a material by vibrations and re-radiated to another point (i.e., upper floor foot traffic). Sound transmission requirements are performance-based.

Spaces that handle classified information must comply with specific criteria to maintain privacy for Sensitive Compartmented Information Facilities (SCIF) or other information-sensitive spaces.

Anti-Terrorism/Force Protection

Data center designed for use by DoD, are required to meet the AT/FP criteria in UFC 4-010-01. DoD buildings are categorized as low occupancy, inhabited, primary gathering, high occupancy family housing, or billeting. A data center would probably be considered low occupancy unless there are large meeting rooms. DoD buildings also must meet requirements for the prevention of progressive collapse. The construction documents must provide the construction information necessary for the evaluation of all applicable DoD standards.

4. INFRASTRUCTURE & UTILITIES

Commercial Power

Commercial power is vitally important because a data center relies heavily on commercial power to operate. While it is true that public utilities and operators of transmission and distribution of electricity are vulnerable to disruption by those wishing to do harm, the fact is that utilities have begun to pay a great deal of attention to preventing disruption (either from physical attack or cyber-physical attack). Needless to say, backup power is an absolute must and multiple redundant backup systems (N+2) are "more better".

How vulnerable is a data center to commercial power outage? *CrashOverRide* malware can control electricity substation switches and circuit breakers, designed decades ago, allowing an attacker to simply turn off power distribution, causing cascading failures and severe damage to electrical equipment. This grid-sabotaging malware was likely used in the December 2016 cyber-attack against the Ukrainian electric utility. *CrashOverRide* is extensible and with a small amount of tailoring such as the inclusion of a DNP3 (Distributed Network Protocol 3) protocol stack would also be effective in the North American grid. *CrashOverRide* can be modified to target other types of critical infrastructure, like transportation, gas lines, or water facilities with additional protocol modules. *CrashOverRide* does not exploit any "zero-day" software vulnerabilities to do its malicious activities; instead, it relies on four industrial communication protocols used worldwide in power supply infrastructure, transportation control systems, and other critical infrastructure systems. *CrashOverRide* can cause wider and longer-lasting blackouts. Also called *Industroyer*.

Redundant Backup Systems

In addition to diesel generators and micro-turbines, data centers are beginning to install redundant backup battery systems such as energy storage systems (ESS) manufactured by Tesla. For example, in response to a four-month long gas leak at Aliso Canyon, California, AltaGas completed and connected its 20MW energy storage system at the Pomona Energy Facility in California in just a few months rather than years. (Note: This case was not a Tesla system.)

The project set an industry record for its rapid turnaround of the design, integration and installation of the system in under four months. The system constitutes North America's largest battery storage facility, comprised of 12,240 lithium-ion batteries in 1,020 racks. It can deliver 80MWh of electricity during peak periods of energy demand to power around 15,000 homes over four hours each day, according to AltaGas.

Whereas this project is representative of "grid-side" or "front-of-the-meter" applications, data centers require "behind-the-meter" installations. As battery pack prices continue their rapid decline, grid-side ESSs will grow in size (from 2MW to 100MW in size). This is because lower battery pack prices make it is a lot easier to justify longer-duration, higher-capacity projects. Of course, I can't resist adding something about renewable energy. Unless your data center was built adjacent to a hydroelectric dam, forget it. The same goes for flywheels. I am skeptical of claims of a 4-hour flywheel, but I have been wrong before. Better to go with lots of diesel generators, micro-turbines and battery storage systems.

Communications Infrastructure

Just as the data center relies on commercial power, they also rely on a robust communications infrastructure. While you can control what happens inside the fence line, you have very little control on what goes on outside the fence line so redundant communications is a must. The possible candidates include dedicated wire or optical fiber systems, conducted power line communications, and/or one or more of the wireless technologies (e.g. narrow band radios, wireless mesh technologies (900 MHz, ZigBee®, etc.), WiFi® and even 4G (WiMAX® or LTE®) as well as microwave and satellite options). Bear in mind the potential sources and levels of interference resulting from interaction with the electromagnetic environment where the communication systems are deployed. The intentional (from wireless or radio systems) or unintentional (from wired systems) radiation from one device may also couple into and interfere with other nearby electronics or receivers.

Dedicated shielded wire or optical fiber (not encased in metal protective covers) systems can offer increased isolation from harsh electromagnetic environments. Wired systems may couple interfering signals onto the connecting wires if not properly shielded and routed away from strong sources. Optical fiber systems eliminate this problem but may experience failure due to dielectric break down of the fiber in especially severe electromagnetic fields. Some installations encase the optical fiber in protective metal jackets or use fiber with internal metallic strengthening materials, which provides EM coupling similar to a metallic wired system. These coupled currents can then enter the electronics connected to the fiber cable. The optical fiber system may be the best solution for many point-to-point higher data rate applications. Proper grounding techniques and installation practices can reduce or eliminate these concerns. The wire and optical fiber systems will both need adequate EMC immunity for the electronics at the endpoints or interfaces.

Domestic Water

Unfortunately, modern HVAC equipment needs a lot of water in order to function properly. Just like the other utilities, redundant backup systems are needed to ensure continuity of operations.

This can be achieved with storage tanks (million gallons), wells and capture of condensate from HVAC systems. Bear in mind that water from some sources need more chemical treatment than others. It is always a good idea to have utility company water access from two connection points, preferably on opposite side of the campus.

Sewage Disposal

Just like the domestic water issue, sewage disposal (and perhaps temporary storage) should be considered to prevent backup of sewage into the building.

Building Equipment Maintenance and Repairs

This is something that has been a pet peeve for a while. Why is it that some data centers locate server room cooling equipment in spaces that require HVAC technicians to enter a high-security server room? Why not locate CRAC units, for example along perimeter walls so that the chilled water line is the only part that is actually in the server room. When the CRAC units need maintenance, the HVAC technicians can work on them from the corridor and need never go into the server room. The fewer people that have access to enter the server rooms, the better.

Provocative Maintenance

This is Hackerspeak for preventative maintenance. These are actions performed upon a machine at regularly scheduled intervals to ensure that the system remains in a usable state. So-called because it is all too often performed by a field technician who doesn't know what he is doing; such 'maintenance' often induces problems, or otherwise results in the machine's remaining in an unusable state for an indeterminate amount of time.

5. DATA CENTER CYBERSECURITY

Today, data centers are spending more on cybersecurity than ever before. At the same time, there are reports of an increasing number of successful cyberattacks by nation states, terrorists, hacktivists, and other bad actors who are stealing our intellectual property, national secrets, and private information. As someone concerned about data center security, I focus on defending the built environment, not protecting the data that resides on servers in the data center. I leave that for others to discuss.

Before discussing anything else, let's look at the data center Security Assurance Level (SAL). This is a requirements-based approach to selection of security controls using the relative consequences of a successful attack against the control system being evaluated. The consequence analysis identifies the worst, reasonable consequence that could be generated by a specific threat scenario. The SAL provides an overall rating of the criticality based on the users' review of security threat scenarios and estimated consequences which is used to establish the potential for harm and loss both onsite and offsite. The SAL ranges from Low to Very High. Low, Moderate, and High correspond with the levels identified by NIST in the NIST SP800-53 standards, the NIST SP800-60 Volumes 1 and 2 documents, and the CFATS risk-based tiering structure. Very High is defined as comprising all controls including all optional enhancements. The Cyber Security Evaluation Tool (CSET) developed by the Department of Homeland Defense is used to determine if a facility meets the target SAL set by an agency. CSET also is used to determine the Mission Assurance Level (MAC) and the Department of Defense **Assurance Level**. This is important to remember if you handle DoD data, or if you ever plan to.

The fundamental cyber-physical security problem can be described in three words—*too much complexity*. Increased complexity translates to increased *attack surface*. There are simply too many flex points—all the software, firmware, and hardware components that we rely on to run the data center infrastructure and controls systems is too complex. In the old days, a boiler was controlled by manually turning valves in the mechanical room. Today, energy management control systems monitor the performance of the boiler and make minute adjustments based on parameters set in the control room which may be miles away from the mechanical room. This might not be as big a problem if the boiler is directly connected to the control room, especially if the boiler manufacturer developed a proprietary boiler control protocol.

Today's boilers (and chillers, and air handlers, and…just about everything else in the mechanical room) rely on a standard protocol running on a standard IP-based network using default passwords that are often unchanged (and, in some cases, manufacturers hard-wire the password so it cannot be changed). This open architecture opens up the data center utility infrastructure to cyber-physical attack. As we say in the military, there are vulnerabilities that are known; vulnerabilities that are unknown; and vulnerabilities created by our adversaries after they have taken control of our system. So, there are vulnerabilities that we can find and fix, and vulnerabilities that we cannot detect.

Cybersecurity efforts start with cyber hygiene. Cyber hygiene activities include: inventory of hardware and software assets; proper configuration of firewalls and other commercial products; scanning for vulnerabilities; patching systems; monitoring and employee training. While good cyber hygiene is necessary, it's not enough. We need to reduce the complexity of the basic architecture and design of the building controls systems and incorporate well-defined engineering-based security design principles at every level.

An effective cyber-attack typically begins with a *Cyber Campaign*. This denotes the time during which a given cyber force conducts a series of planned and coordinated cyber-attacks or other Cyber Operations in a given network environment (sometimes referred to as the "NEO", *Network Environment of Operation*). A cyber campaign may be executed by either a single actor, or as a combined effort of multiple actors. A cyber campaign is a series of related cyber operations aimed towards a single, specific, strategic objective or result. A cyber campaign may take place over the course of just a few days or weeks, or it can last several months or years.

Cyber-Collection refers to the use of cyber-warfare techniques in order to conduct espionage. Cyber-collection activities typically rely on the insertion of malware into a targeted network or computer in order to scan for, collect and exfiltrate sensitive information. Local and network storage are scanned to find and copy files of interest, these are often documents, spreadsheets, design files such as Autocad files and system files such as the password file. Cyber-collection started as far back as 1996, when widespread deployment of Internet connectivity to government and corporate systems gained momentum. Since that time, there have been numerous cases of such activity. In addition to the state sponsored examples, cyber-collection has also been used by organized crime for identity and e-banking theft and by corporate spies.

A persistent attacker will prepare a *Cyber Attack Tree*. This is a conceptual diagram showing how a computer system might be attacked by describing the threats and possible cyber-attacks to realize those threats. Cyber-attack trees lend themselves to defining an information assurance strategy and are increasingly being applied to industrial control systems and the electric power grid. Executing a defensive strategy that can be detected by the attacker changes the cyber-attack tree. There are at least 150 ways to attack a BCS that I am aware of.

Cyber-Attack Vectors

Cyber-attacks are broken down into two categories:
- **Syntactic attacks** are straight forward; it is considered malicious software which includes viruses, worms and Trojan horses.
- **Semantic attack** is the modification and dissemination of correct and incorrect information. Information modification could be done without the use of computers though new opportunities can be found daily. This can be used by an attacker to set forensics in the wrong direction or to cover their tracks through dissemination of incorrect information.

Cyber-Infiltration - There are several common ways to infect the data center building controls system or access the target:
- An **Injection Proxy** is a system that is placed upstream from the target individual or company, usually at the Internet service provider, that injects malware into the targets system. For example, an innocent download made by the user can be injected with the malware executable on the fly so that the target system then is accessible to crackers.

- **Spear Phishing**: A carefully crafted e-mail is sent to the target in order to entice them to install the malware via a Trojan document or a drive by attack hosted on a web server compromised or controlled by the malware owner.
- **Surreptitious Entry** may be used to infect a system. In other words, the spies carefully break into the target's office and install the malware on the target's system.
- An **Upstream monitor** or sniffer is a device that can intercept and view the data transmitted by a target system. Usually this device is placed at the Internet Service Provider. The Carnivore system is a famous example of this type of system. Based on the same logic as a telephone intercept, this type of system is of limited use today due to the widespread use of encryption during data transmission.
- A **wireless infiltration** system can be used in proximity of the target when the target is using wireless technology. This is usually a laptop-based system that impersonates a Wi-Fi or 3G base station to capture the target systems and relay requests upstream to the Internet. Once the target systems are on the network, the system then functions as an Injection Proxy or as an Upstream Monitor in order to infiltrate or monitor the target system. If you use wireless devices on your BCS, it has already been scanned and mapped.
- A **USB Key** preloaded with the malware infector may be given to or dropped at the target site. Also, called a Rubber Ducky.
- **Internet Access** - If your BCS is connected to the Internet, your network has already been scanned and mapped.
- **Insider Threat** - Deliberate or inadvertent activity.
- **Direct-Access** Attack - Gaining physical access to a BCS network device.
- **Rogue wireless access point** on the BCS network (inadvertent or intentional).
- **Removable Media** - USB, floppy, CD, laptop, anything that can connect directly to a BCS network device.
- **Email** - Malware delivered by phishing email such as a virus, Trojan horse, worm.
- **Other Networks** - A connection to the corporate enterprise network can be one way to get into the BCS.
- **Supply Chain** - If it's made overseas, it's probably got some hidden program you'll never find.
- **Improper Installation or Usage** - Deliberate or inadvertent activity.
- **Theft of Equipment** - Lose a vital piece of equipment and your system can be left defenseless.
- **Cyber-Drone** - An aerial drone can monitor a building seeking wireless signals, such as from network printers with default passwords.
- **Other** - Whatever I left out.

What is a *Cyber-Drone*? A cyber-drone can carry lightweight but powerful hacking platforms like Wi-Fi Pineapple and Raspberry Pi, packaged with an external battery pack and cellular connection, for powerful eavesdropping and man-in-the-middle attacks. A cyber-drone (or a swarm) can search for Wi-Fi wireless networks connected to a BCS at a facility and hack into networks when they are found. A cyber-drone can fly outside a data center and find vulnerable networks with minimal interference. For example, a cyber-drone can land on a roof and target wireless printers because they often are the weak link in a company's network. Wireless printers are typically supplied with the Wi-Fi connection open by default, and many companies are unaware or forget to close this hole when they add the device to their Wi-Fi networks. This open connection potentially provides an access point for outsiders to connect to the BCS network. It is also possible for a cyber-drone to shut down computer systems and other nearby electronic systems from the sky through targeted emission of microwaves.

Anti-drone technology is beginning to come on the market for WLAN customers as cyber-drones become attached to more verified network attacks. Fluke Networks has released the first cyber-drone detection signature as an update to its *AirMagnet Enterprise* wireless IDS/IPS product that alerts customers to drone-specific signals. Cyber-drones are controlled via an ad hoc network and *AirMagnet* can detect the command-and-control signaling. The *AirMagnet* also can detect video transmission streams. Once alerted, the network administrator can either attempt to locate the drone and its operator or take RF or WLAN system-level countermeasures.

Is it possible to plug all those holes? Maybe not, but why make it easy for them to get in? Let's assume they've already scanned and mapped your building controls network. We all know firewalls can easily be defeated. We also know that if your building controls are connected to the internet, a attacker doesn't even need to install a virus or other malware to wreak havoc.

Phishing

This is the preferred method for most cyber-attacks. In its simplest terms, phishing is tricking individuals into disclosing sensitive personal information by claiming to be a trustworthy entity in an electronic communication (e.g., Internet web sites). Phishing typically involves both social engineering and technical trickery to deceive victims into opening attached files, clicking on embedded links, and revealing sensitive information. An *in-session* phishing attack uses a pop-up to launch a fake browser window that pretends to have been opened from the targeted session (such as a banking web site). This pop-up window, which the victim now believes to be part of the targeted session, is then used to steal user data in the same way as with other phishing attacks.

Whether it's a phishing email containing a *decoy document* that executes malware on a victim's device that's sent to hundreds of in-boxes, or targeted spear phishing doesn't really matter if it happens to you. Let's assume that someone at the data center is specifically targeted by an attacker wishing to disrupt operations. The attacker will gather as much personal information about their victim as possible with the sole purpose of obtaining unauthorized access to the victim's sensitive data such as network access credentials. Any information uploaded to social media sites like FaceBook and Linked-In can be very useful to an attacker planning to disrupt data center operations. Phishing is, by far, the most successful vector on the Internet today, accounting for **91% of cyber-attacks**.

As if that weren't bad enough, phishing is getting more sophisticated. Most computer-savvy employees can spot obvious phishing emails when they are shotgun-type broadcast to the world, but automated spear phishing is increasingly laser-focused - 77 percent of the verified attacks targeted only 10 mailboxes or less while one-third (33 percent) targeted just one single mailbox. Automated laser phishing is using artificial intelligence to scan things like our social media presences, and craft false but believable messages from people we know, to create a believable imitation of them using publicly available information. A *whaling attack* is spear phishing targeting high-profile executives, politicians and celebrities. Whaling emails are highly-personalized and appear to come from a trusted source. Once opened, the target is directed to a website that was created specifically for that individual's attack. Successful whaling targets are referred to as having been "harpooned".

Unfortunately, a Computerized Maintenance Management System (CMMS) depends heavily on connectivity to the Internet as well as wireless communications to work efficiently. Building maintenance personnel are notified by the CMMS when equipment needs attention such as when a pump or valve malfunctions by generating and sending a work order to a mobile device. Maintenance personnel can access information wirelessly such as past maintenance history, preventive maintenance performed, all the specifications for the device including capacity, normal operating parameters and even whether spare parts are on hand and where they are located in the storage room. Some CMMS databases include tenant information such as who requested maintenance, the room number and telephone number. Some CMMS databases contain information such as security clearance for staff, labor rates, vacation schedule and contact information. The CMMS would be a great tool to target maintenance personnel for spear phishing attacks.

When a cracker breaks into the CMMS, he can see a great deal of information about the building and how it is operated. A cracker can see which pieces of equipment are high-priority assets, determine which equipment can be considered safety hazards and discover the trigger points for failure alarms and automatic shutdowns. A cracker can even see whether spare parts are on hand so he can target equipment that would take longer to repair. Another thing to consider is that the CMMS is typically tied directly to the BCS network making the CMMS a possible attack vector for crackers.

An attacker can also use a *Smishing Attack*. This is a form of phishing attack that uses a cell phone text message (SMS) to lure a target to a website or prompting the target to a call a telephone number in an attempt to persuade target to reveal information such as pin number. Often a smishing victim is informed he will be charged for something unless he clicks on a link and cancels it. Some attackers use short links on phishing emails designed to look like Gmail alerts containing a short link that led to a fake webpage to harvest the victim's password. Some used Google's own style and look for a security alert. To a distracted or untrained eye, there would be no difference between this and the real thing.

Then there is also the *Vishing Attack*. This is a type of phishing attack that uses a telephone ("v" is for voice) to obtain personal information. Phishing target is called directly by criminals or receives an email asking the target to call a specific phone number.

The point here is that the computer employees need to be trained to spot a phishing attack and anyway, the computer used for email at the data center should not be connected to the building controls network. It's just too risky.

Malware

Not all cyber-attacks rely on loading malware on a target system. A *fileless cyber-attack* uses inherent "features" built into Windows to turn the operating system against itself to compromise a computer network. The best examples are using *Windows Management Instrumentation* (WMI) and *Powershell*. WMI has access to every resource on the machine and can perform various tasks such as execute files, delete and copy files, or change registry values. Powershell is an even more powerful tool for crackers. Some new fileless malware types reside in an encrypted form in the Windows registry hive. Kovter, Powelike, and XswKit are fileless registry attack malware that destroys itself upon execution and leave no trace on the file system. This disappearing malware resides only in the infected machine's random-access-memory, rather than on the hard drive, so that the malware leaves no discernible footprint once it's gone. WMI cannot be uninstalled (but it can be disabled). Since no other software needs to be installed, a fileless attack is nearly impossible for traditional antivirus tools to detect. Tracking fileless attacks may be difficult, but it's not impossible using memory forensics techniques.

Industroyer Malware - The malicious toolkit developed for ICS-specific cyber-physical attacks against electric utilities that is expressly coded to be an automated, grid-killing weapon. Four ICS-specific modules operate in conjunction with one another to exploit four communications protocols used in Europe, Asia and most of the Middle East known as IEC 101, IEC 104, IEC 61850, and OLE for Process Control Data Access (OPC DA). Industroyer includes two backdoors, used to gain persistence on systems (the second backdoor is designed to regain access if the first backdoor is detected or disabled); a wiper component for erasing critical system files to render grid operator stations inoperable; and a port scanner to map infected networks during the reconnaissance stage. Industroyer has to be custom-built for each target using a configuration that is specific to that site. Also, called CrashOverride.

Attackers have been known to use *Process Doppelgänging* - using two key distinct features to mask the loading of a modified executable. Malicious code that utilizes Process Doppelgänging is never saved to disk (fileless attack), which makes it invisible to all major security products. Similar to process hollowing, it utilizes the Windows mechanism of NTFS Transactions. Advanced forensics tools such as *Volatility* will not detect it.

Industrial Controls Systems

What is a cyber-physical attack? A cyber-physical attack is one in which a wholly digital attack against Cyber-Physical Systems (CPS) caused physical destruction of equipment. A cyber-physical attack is different from an enterprise network cyber-attack designed to steal money, exfiltrate information, or hold a computer hostage for ransom. Those attacks are fairly simple and can be carried out by a cyber-criminal, or even a garden variety cracker (NOTE: A "cracker" is a hacker with malicious intent. The terms are not interchangeable). All hackers are NOT crackers.

Cyber-Physical Systems are engineered systems that are built from, and depend upon, the seamless integration of computational algorithms and physical components. Traditional analysis tools are unable to cope with the full complexity of CPS or adequately predict system behavior.

As the Internet of Things (IoT) scales to billions of connected devices - with the capacity to sense, control, and otherwise interact with the human and physical world - the requirements for dependability, security, safety, and privacy grow immensely. One barrier to progress is the lack of appropriate science and technology to conceptualize and design for the deep interdependencies among engineered systems and the natural world.

Hacking into a Building Controls Systems (BCS), Industrial Controls Systems (ICS), and Supervisory Controls and Data Acquisition (SCADA) networks is not the same as breaking into enterprise networks that process information. BCS, ICS and SCADA systems are much more complex. Breaking into a controls system is only a means to an end. The target is not the network itself, it is the equipment being controlled.

Below is a partial list of cyber-attack hazards capable of being carried out via BCS systems to disrupt data center functions (single or multiple cyber-attack vectors simultaneously).
- Denial-of-service, force continual equipment hardware reboots
- Shut off building utilities (electric, water, sewage pumps)
- Turn equipment off or continuously cycle rapidly
- Sever data center communications
- Take security and alarm systems off-line (CCTV, sensors)
- Change operating parameters (temperature, outside air ventilation levels)
- Set off false alarms
- Display phantom error messages on BCS
- Delete or overwrite data files
- Erase or corrupt system memory (change set points)
- Conceal activity on the network
- Overspin motors and pumps
- Hide valid equipment failure notifications
- Change user passwords (privilege escalation)
- Lock out maintenance personnel from BCS access
- Contaminate potable water supply (backflow)
- Crash all systems simultaneously and change network configuration

Although designing a catastrophic cyber-physical attack scenario to exploit a particular physical process requires a solid engineering background and in-depth destructive knowledge of the target controls system (Cyber-Physical Attack Engineering) --- you don't need an engineering background to figure out how to turn equipment off.

In addition, a typical ICS contains multiple control loops and sometimes the control loops are nested and/or cascading, so the set point for one loop is based on the process variable output from another loop. Interrupting one process can have a ripple effect through the factory. Supervisory control loops and lower-level loops operate continuously over the duration of a process with cycle times of milliseconds.

A cracker doesn't need to have an engineering degree to figure out that a large change in the setpoint (or process values) on a proportional feedback system will have a larger effect than a small change that would be tolerated based on the sensitivity of the control system and the process. But, even a small change that results in sluggish response in the short-term could have a major effect over a relatively long period of time.

The only saving grace in an industrial environment is that a newbie or script kiddie will not thoroughly understand complex manufacturing processes. While a newbie may be able to turn off the lights in the factory, I doubt he would know how to increase the deadband (an interval of a signal domain where no action occurs - the system is 'dead' - i.e. the output is zero) on voltage regulators or cause repeated activation-deactivation cycles.

Hacking a chemical plant to create a weapon of mass destruction (a Bhopal-style catastrophic failure) for example, requires knowledge of physics, chemistry and engineering, as well as a great deal about how the network is laid out, and a keen understanding of process-aware defensive systems. The most a newbie could hope to do is to turn something off. A novice would not know what a Cascade Control Loop is. In a single-loop control, the controller's setpoint is set by an operator, and its output drives a final control element. For example, a level controller driving a control valve to keep the level at its setpoint. In a cascade control arrangement, there are two (or more) controllers of which one controller's output drives the setpoint of another controller such as a level controller driving the setpoint of a flow controller to keep the level at its setpoint. The flow controller, in turn, drives a control valve to match the flow with the setpoint the level controller is requesting. The controller driving the setpoint (the level controller) is called the primary, outer, or master controller. The controller receiving the setpoint (flow controller) is called the secondary, inner or slave controller. A cascade control loop is used when a process with relatively slow dynamics (like level, temperature, composition, humidity) and a liquid or gas flow, or some other relatively-fast process, has to be manipulated to control the slow process.

A well-qualified attacker (such as a foreign security service) hitting a data center building controls network seeks to take control over the equipment. Those crackers understand the equipment they will be controlling. No offense but, most IT guys are not familiar with electrical and mechanical equipment, industrial and manufacturing equipment, or utility equipment, so they wouldn't know how to defend them. That's because they don't know the equipment or processes being controlled.

The same is true of the folks in charge of physical security at these facilities. The typical security guys don't know anything about electrical and mechanical systems, or how computer networks are designed. Let's face it, they don't have the budget or the training to deal with these new threats.

The owner is looking to the facility guys, the IT guys and the security guys to work together to defend their physical plant, and in many cases, these guys aren't even talking to each other. Most of the time, they think cyber-physical security is someone else's responsibility! In essence, "nobody is minding the store". An effective defense against cyber-physical attacks requires procedural safeguards, such as frequent password changes, equipment inspections, random drills, security awareness programs, records retention programs, etc.

So, what is the big deal? On December 3 1984, in Bhopal, India there was an industrial accident at a pesticide plant that immediately killed at least 3,800 people and caused significant morbidity and premature death for many thousands more. That was only one incident with a release of only 40 tons of methyl isocyanate gas. Of course, this was an accident and not a cyber-physical attack, but it should give you an idea what could happen in a worst-case scenario.

Another example is what actually happened at a Chrysler assembly plant. An attacker shut down one auto plant with a worm that quickly spread to all other Chrysler plants, idling 50,000 workers. These were professionally-installed industrial control networks with firewalls and safety features. I suspect they were protected in much the same way that many enterprise networks are protected today.

The bad news is that crackers are getting better at what they do. In the good old days, an attacker would use a virus or worm to take over your computer. Nowadays they can attack your computer without loading any files at all. That's because all the files they need to take over are already loaded on your computer. That's called a Fileless Cyber-Attack. All they need to do is trick you into giving them permission to access those files. Anti-virus software has gotten very good at detecting and stopping a computer virus. Attackers find it much easier to fool a human using social engineering.

Data center facilities and infrastructure maintenance personnel need to understand the vulnerability of their building controls systems to cyber-physical attack. This book includes simple descriptions of some of the vulnerabilities (attack vectors) of automated equipment controls common to data centers. The book also lists different types of cyber-physical attacks discovered.

Alarm Notifications - BCS alarms tend to fall into one of four categories:
    True Positive – Something bad happened and the IDS caught it.
    True Negative – The event is benign and no alert was generated.
    False Positive – The IDS alert sounded, but the event was not malicious.
    False Negative - Something bad happened, the IDS didn't catch it.

Traditional IT-focused security solutions are unsuitable for equipment control networks such as a BCS. A BCS uses computers to monitor performance of equipment, sensors and devices and adjusts device parameters to accommodate changes due to weather or building occupancy. Even under normal network traffic, broadcast messages can overload some building equipment controls and cause them to crash. Making a data center cyber-secure may be easier than securing IT-focused networks, because although you cannot stop all viruses from infecting a computer, you can stop an infected computer from damaging building equipment.

Various equipment vendors have developed network security "appliances" that create zones of security as recommended by ISA/IEC-62443 Standards. For example, the *Xenon Security Appliance* manufactured by *Tofino, Inc.* is installed into an existing network with no changes to the network, forming "conduits" of communications between zones. If a cyber-attack originates from a secondary entry point, the potential damage is contained within the zone in which the attack originated and does not spread across the entire network.

Tofino SA

The controls engineer defines rules that specify which network devices are allowed to communicate and what protocols they may use. Any network traffic that does not fit the rules is automatically blocked by the appliance and reported as a security alert. Deep packet inspection allows detailed filters to enforce security policy, such as only allowing read commands to be sent to a programmable logic controller.

How Can a Cyber-Attack Disrupt Data Center Operations?

Steam Boilers

A "boiler" is a closed pressure vessel in which water or other fluid (hydronic) is used to heat a building, while a "furnace" uses warm air. The heat is different, and the way that heat is circulated through the building is different. Once in your BCS, a hacker can send any one of many locking and blocking error codes to the boiler to shut it down. Interrupting the fuel that feeds the boiler or furnace or interfering with the combustion process are both problematic, at best, but a boiler that has a loss of feed water and is permitted to boil dry can be extremely dangerous. If feed water is then sent into that empty boiler, the small cascade of incoming water instantly boils on contact with the superheated metal shell and leads to a violent explosion that cannot be controlled even by steam safety valves.

Boiler Sequence Controller Hack

Boiler controller, burner programmer, burner controller, sequence controller, and programmable sequence controllers, measure the temperature of the combined water flow of a multi-boiler installation. They are pre-programmed for the automatic operation of gas/oil burners and regulate how many boilers operate to match the required demand. They continuously monitor the flame and can control how many boilers fire up at one time for safe start-up. They provide output for blower, ignition, solenoid valves with prefixed timing for continuous flame supervision. Hack this and all the boilers can be turned on full blast.

Hot Water Heater Explosion

Fire departments are familiar with the explosive potential of a hot-water heater. If a hacker can cause the hot-water heater tank (a pressure vessel) to flash into explosive failure at 332°F, the explosion will hurl burning debris in all directions with tremendous force. Equipment several rooms from the point of the explosion become airborne and people in the mechanical room can be injured or killed as the water heater explodes. It is important to remember that the blast from an explosion in a mechanical room will travel through building ductwork and I have seen air vents on the other side of a building blown out from a blast event.

Chillers

Chillers are not as dangerous as steam boilers or pressure vessels, but a hacker can wreak havoc with your chillers if he knows what he's doing. The old absorption chillers generated Hydrogen gas naturally as a result of the reaction of Lithium Bromide with the steel surfaces of chiller, but they are not very common anymore. A hacker attempting to disrupt the chilled water system will generally tamper with the refrigerant flow or the condenser water temperature. If a hacker can cause the pressure differential (lift) to exceed the capacity of the compressor, the backward pressure flow will cause the chiller to surge. Conversely, if the hacker can cause the pressure in the evaporator to drop, that can also cause the compressor to surge. If the compressor surges, you will know it because it is very noisy and it will trip the breaker.

The cooling tower can also cause the compressor to surge with reduction in the flow of water to the condenser. If the cooling tower fan stops, you will get a high temperature condition. Of course, the hacker would have to defeat the low temperature safety switch, so it does not shut down the chiller automatically. Chiller surge will cause damage to the rotating assemblies. When a second or lag machine must be started, the timing of the isolation valves is crucial in preventing a surge condition. If the valve does not open after 90 seconds, the lag system automatically shuts back down in a failure mode.

If a hacker shuts down the chiller and leaves the pump on, the water in the system heats up increasing the pressure on the cooling side of the chiller. That will increase the pressure in the chamber causing the rupture disc to fail, releasing the refrigerant into the atmosphere. If the refrigerant is R-11, maintenance personnel can be overcome, and being unable to breathe, possibly pass out from lack of oxygen. This is not the case with R-34 refrigerant. Of course, repairing the rupture disc and replacing lost refrigerant will take time and you should be back up and running in a couple days (provided you have a preferred maintenance agreement with the building equipment vendor).

Cooling Towers

A cooling tower is used to dispose of unwanted heat from a chiller. Water-cooled chillers operating on the principle of evaporative cooling are normally more energy-efficient than air-cooled chillers. To achieve better performance (more cooling), they are designed to increase the surface area and the time of contact between the air and water flow. A "collection basin" is used to collect and contain the cooled water after its interaction with the air flow. Make-up water is added to the system to compensate for water lost due to evaporation.

Cooling tower water is filtered to remove particulates and treated with biocides and algaecides to prevent growths that could interfere with the continuous flow of the water and prevent the growth of Legionella, including species that cause legionellosis or Legionnaires' Disease, most notably L. pneumophila, or Mycobacterium avium. Cooling towers are fitted with electrical immersion heaters, steam coils or hot water coils in the collection basin to prevent freezing. Obviously, the basin heater should not be operating in the summer as that would contribute to growth of opportunistic pathogens.

Modern cooling towers are designed with a drift eliminator that provides multiple directional changes of airflow to prevent the escape of water droplets. They are designed to prevent excessively high water levels and possible overflow of the cold water basin due to over pumping, clogged strainers, or makeup valve malfunction.

A hacker wishing to disrupt a building HVAC may decide to flood the cooling tower collection basin, turn off the fans and heat the water in the basin. Turning off the pumps or intermittent fan reversal would also cause damage to the cooling tower, chillers or both. Another hack would be to search the installation files to determine the resonant operation speed of the unit that may result in vibrations which could damage the components or structure, and/or create objectionable noise. The resonant speed ranges are identified at start-up and typically locked out to prevent the variable frequency drive to operate the motor at these resonant speeds. A hacker may also interfere with the chemical "pot" feeder that injects diluted liquid biocides directly to the collection water basin.

Another possible hack would be to spoof the Vibration Cutout Switch (VCOS) to shut down the cooling tower. A VCOS is designed to cause a trip condition when it detects any vibration after a time delay. A VCOS can be mechanical or electronic with a single setpoint containing one trip limit for alarm or shut down.

Backup Generator

In 2007, CNN broadcast a demonstration of an "AURORA" cyber-physical attack of a 2.25 Mega Watt diesel generator connected to a substation that ended with an explosion that sent engine parts flying as far as 80 feet. This test was conducted at the Idaho National Laboratory (INL) for the Department of Homeland Security (DHS). INL staff injected a virus consisting of 20 lines of code that caused an out-of-phase condition that can damage alternating current (AC) equipment connected to the power grid.

Connecting AC equipment out-of-phase is a known vulnerability, but doing it maliciously was brought to light by the test conducted by INL. This condition occurs when a circuit breaker or breakers are opened and closed rapidly, resulting in an out-of-phase condition. The test demonstrated the threat associated with rapidly disconnecting and reconnecting a generator to the grid, but out of phase - via physical or cyber intrusion of control systems conducted maliciously or unintentionally.

Because an AURORA event consists of the out-of-sync reconnecting of three-phase rotating equipment, that means that just about any three-phase equipment (motors, generators) can be attacked. Risk mitigation is achieved by placing a hardware device that monitors for the rapid out-of-phase condition associated with an AUORA event between each substation and its loads. The device isolates the substation from its loads before the torque of the grid can be applied to the equipment. Two relay protection suppliers manufacture a Digital Protection and Control Devices (DPCD) capable of closing breakers that can adversely impact critical electrical rotating equipment: Cooper Power Systems, and Schweitzer Engineering Laboratories. They are relatively inexpensive and have wiring configurations similar to other relays.

A hacker can break into the BCS through an enterprise network Access Point (A device that logically connects wireless client devices operating in the building infrastructure to one another and provides access to a distribution system, if connected, which is typically a data center's enterprise wired network).

A hacker that can access your BCS can use Alarm Flooding (annunciation of more alarms in a given period of time than a human operator can respond) to confuse maintenance personnel. Ten alarms per minute is typically the most alarms a technician can handle.

The price of connectivity is less security. The more connected a device is, the less secure it will be. If there is only one thing you get out of this book, it should be this: Data center building controls should not be connected to the Internet – unless the intended purpose is to have them hacked and out of action.

Preventing Cyber-Physical Attacks

Perfect cyber-security is unachievable, and probably unaffordable. However, there are steps you can take to reduce the risk of *cyber-physical attack* against buildings, manufacturing facilities and utilities. First, make sure the BCS uses smart controls. **Smart controls** use communications based on the Ethernet protocol making field devices not only self-aware of its status by raising an alarm when a condition occurs that may cause performance to deteriorate, but also system-aware as an autonomous automation asset capable of interacting with others within a network. An example is a variable speed drive motor controlling pumps and actuators. The drive is able to learn a pump operating profile to find an optimized operational point for the pump depending on flow or pressure.

Physical Access to the Hardware

Let me begin by saying that unless you implement stringent physical access controls, the rest of what I am about to tell you will be in vain. Cyber assets and their communication media should be protected 100% of the time with a six-wall border to limit physical tampering with the systems and media. Not only should access doors have locks, the doors should automatically close. Do not allow employees to prop doors open for any reason.

An attacker begins by *footprinting* the target facility. He sifts through *open-source* material found on the Internet to learn all he can about the target, including who works there, what equipment is there, and where it is located. An attacker may visit the building, sniff the wireless spectrum, look in dumpsters, and use *social engineering* to assemble a very good picture of the target network and its equipment to determine where the vulnerabilities are.

Ofttimes, I've been able to wander into a *Building Control Center* without being challenged. All I need is a construction helmet and a clip board. In fact, there are professional *hackers* called **Sneakers** that specialize in finding ways to penetrate a physical security barrier.

To compound the problem, most of the time people sitting at a workstation connected to the BCS network don't even log out when they leave the room. Anyone can sit at the workstation and sabotage the equipment when the user steps out. A visitor wishing to compromise network security need only plug a **Rubber Ducky**, **LAN Turtle** or **Bash Bunny** into a USB port and the system is "*pwned*".

HackRF - A USB-powered Software Defined Radio peripheral capable of transmission or reception of radio signals from 10 MHz to 6 GHz.

Rubber Ducky - *A Keystroke Injection Attack Platform* hidden in a USB thumb drive. Whether it be a Windows, Mac, Linux or Android device, any *USB* device claiming to be a *Keyboard HID* will be automatically detected and accepted by most modern operating systems. By taking advantage of this inherent trust with scripted keystrokes (at speeds beyond 1000 words per minute), traditional countermeasures can be bypassed.

LAN Turtle - A covert *Penetration Testing* tool providing *stealth remote access, network intelligence gathering, and man-in-the-middle* surveillance capabilities through a simple graphic shell. A *cracker* can use this to:
- Scan the network using nmap
- DNS Spoof clients to phishing sites
- Exfiltrate data via SSHFS
- Access the entire LAN through a site-to-site *VPN* with the *LAN Turtle* acting as gateway

Bash Bunny - A *USB drive* that emulates combinations of trusted USB devices — like *gigabit Ethernet, serial, flash storage* and *keyboards* so computers are tricked into divulging data, exfiltrating documents, installing backdoors and many more *exploits*. Slide the switch to your payload of choice, plug the *Bash Bunny* into the victim computer and watch the multi-color LED. With a quad-core CPU and desktop-class SSD it goes from *plug to pwn* in 7 seconds.

If the attacker has lots of time, he can install a **Throwing Star LAN Tap.**

LAN Tap - A *passive Ethernet tap*, requiring no power for operation. To the target network, the LAN Tap looks just like a section of cable, but the wires in the cable extend to the monitoring ports in addition to connecting one target port to the other. The *Throwing Star LAN Tap's* monitoring ports (J3 and J4) are receive-only; they connect to the receive data lines on the monitoring station, but do not connect to the network's transmit lines. This makes it impossible for the monitoring station to accidentally transmit data packets onto the target network.

If the attacker has to work quickly, he can insert a **Ralink** into a USB port in the back of a computer. That would turn the computer into a wide-open *backdoor* to the network, with little chance of being discovered.

Ralink - An incredibly small USB Wi-Fi adapter. These are nearly impossible to spot unless you are looking for them. Also, some USB ports are <u>inside</u> the computer case.

If the attacker has lots of time and needs longer range, he can plug a **Wi-Fi Pineapple** into any USB port. It's so small it's not that difficult to hide. It would be tough to spot-unless someone knows it shouldn't be there,

Wi-Fi Pineapple - An advanced wireless device used for *penetration testing* or used by *crackers* as a *rogue access point* for *reconnaissance*, *man-in-the-middle*, *tracking*, *logging* and *reporting*. Not only would the attacker be able to collect/monitor data, he would also be able to modify control **setpoints**. It provides a common interface to wireless sensors and switches. These are not secure and are easily compromised by any garden-variety *cracker*, junior-grade.

For short range communications, a *cracker* can install a **Ubertooth One.** These are a little larger, so are easier to spot – if you are looking for them.

Ubertooth One - An opensource *Bluetooth* test tool from Michael Ossmann. An affordable platform that can be used for *Bluetooth monitoring*. Also used for the development of new *Bluetooth* and wireless technologies.

YARD Stick (Yet Another Radio Dongle) - A USB device that can transmit or receive digital wireless signals at frequencies below 1 GHz.

Be on the lookout for a **Keystroke Logger Attack.** A program or USB device designed to record which keys are pressed on a computer keyboard used to obtain passwords or encryption keys and thus bypass other security measures. A **Mouse Logger** works much the same way.

Any of these tools will allow a *cracker* to alter *setpoints* to raise the limits outside the intended design parameters of the equipment manufacturer. A **Setpoint** (also *set point*) is the desired or target value for an essential variable of a system to describe a standard configuration or norm for the system. For example, a boiler might have a *temperature setpoint*, which is the temperature the boiler control system aims to maintain. This attack is called a **Setpoint Override.**

Most *setpoint* loads in a heating system operate year-round at temperatures above the reset operating temperature. When the *setpoint* load requires heat, this overrides the *Warm Weather Shut Down and Reset* temperature of the control. This function allows the heating system to operate only at the temperature required to satisfy the current load.

End points (CD-ROM, USB, RJ-45, RS-232, RS-485, LON connectors, terminal block connections, serial and parallel ports, jacks, plugs, etc.) should be monitored for security state, attempted access violations, malicious behavior and vulnerabilities. Install *end point protections* on the servers, control consoles and all IP-enabled devices to prevent *Stuxnet*-like intrusion from *insiders* purposefully or haplessly installing *malware* from USB drives (or from installing external attack code that made it onto the BCS network).

Detection devices should be used to identify any attempt to sctup *rogue communication devices*, new systems, connectivity, applications and wireless access. Maintain a list of *approved BCS devices* and the connectivity and communication profiles between devices.

Enforce strict controls and *separation of duties* for direct access and monitoring of control room operators, administrators and others with direct access. I recommend you implement the **Two-Person Control** whenever possible.

> **Two-Person Control -** Continuous surveillance and control of positive control material at all times by a minimum of two authorized individuals, each capable of detecting incorrect and unauthorized procedures with respect to the task being performed and each familiar with established security and safety requirements.
>
> **Two-Person Integrity -** System of storage and handling designed to prohibit individual access by requiring the presence of at least two authorized individuals, each capable of detecting incorrect or unauthorized security procedures with respect to the task being performed. See *no-lone zone*.

Enforce limits on access and hold individuals accountable for their actions. Do not ignore security policy rule violations. Ensure employees are only granted the least privileges necessary to do their jobs. The security objective of **Least Privilege** is to grant users only the access they need to perform their official duties. Studies have shown that in 2016, 47 percent of analyzed organizations had at least 1,000 sensitive files open to every employee; and 22 percent had 12,000 sensitive files open to every employee.

Equipment vendors will want to bring along a laptop to plug into your BCS system to check the performance of their equipment. Again, this is for their convenience and will degrade your security. Do not allow a vendor to connect his laptop computer to the BCS unless absolutely necessary.

If you must, let them use your laptop and test their programs by use of a **sandbox** on a test network (**Digital Twin**). A sandbox is a security mechanism to execute untested or untrusted programs or code, from unverified or untrusted third parties, suppliers, users or websites, without risking harm to the BCS network. A *sandbox* provides a tightly controlled set of resources for guest programs to run in (not a virtual host, separate network). Network access, the ability to inspect the host system or read from input devices are NEVER allowed and ALWAYS heavily restricted. Make sure every laptop computer gets a thorough cleaning and is scanned before and after use for *malware* and *spyware*.

Do not permit wireless control of devices by anyone from inside or outside the building. Whenever possible, use *point-to-point* connections. This includes your own employees. This is a vulnerability that can open all kinds of doors. Keep *smart phones* out of secure areas, except in an emergency.

> Today, most *smartphones* from Verizon Wireless have a built-in **mobile hotspot** function—allowing you to access the Internet anytime. A laptop can also be set up as a *mobile hot spot*.

The point here is that there are many ways to compromise a Building Controls System if you have *physical access* to the hardware. There are many, many access points already on site. A data center is probably the most vulnerable because every room has a *network access point* that anybody can plug into.

Some *cyber-physical attacks* cannot be carried out without access to the physical hardware on site. So, why make it easier for an attacker by leaving the doors unlocked? In fact, you even need to secure your trash bins because *crackers* have been known to resort to **Dumpster Diving.**

> **Dumpster Diving** - Obtaining passwords and a data center's directories by searching through discarded trash bin. Also, referred to as *"skipping."*

Common Sense Physical Security Tips:

- Provide lockable rooms or locking enclosures for all system components (e.g., servers, clients, and networking hardware) and for the systems used to manage and control physical access (e.g., servers, lock controllers, and alarm control panels).
- Provide a method for *tamper detection* on lockable or locking enclosures.
- Change locks, locking codes, keycards, and any other keyed entrances when after any building construction or renovation.
- Reprogram codes (e.g., remove default codes) on locks and locking devices so that the codes/passwords are unique and do not repeat codes used in the past.
- Install network cabling that is routed thru unprotected areas only in metal conduit (that can be visually inspected easily).
- Provide *two-factor authentication* for physical access control.
- Have the BCS equipment supplier certify and provide documentation that communication channels are as direct as possible (e.g., communication paths between devices in one network security zone do not pass through devices maintained at a low security level or cross unnecessarily into low security zones).
- Remove or disable all services and ports not required for normal operation, emergency operations, or troubleshooting. This includes communication ports and physical input/output ports (e.g., USB docking ports, CD/DVD drives, video ports, and serial ports). Inventory and document disabled ports, connectors, and interfaces.
- Install an Uninterruptable Power Supply for all computer equipment.
- Set the BIOS to only boot from the C drive.

Most company's Building Controls Systems (BCS) are connected to the Internet in one way or another. Sometimes, the owner *thinks* the BCS is not connected because the network diagram doesn't show any connections. What the owner doesn't know is that over the years, vendors installed *rogue access points* so they can monitor performance of their equipment remotely. Unfortunately, the owner has lost control of the network security without even knowing they are vulnerable.

Other times, somebody installed a *printer* on the network without knowing it has a *wireless card* in it (or *fax*). They didn't ask for wireless printing capability, so they are unaware that it defaulted to "On" when the printer was installed (or when the power goes off) so the *default password* (usually "password") was never changed. An attacker searching for vulnerabilities will easily detect the wireless printer and use that opening to attack the BCS network.

Some equipment is too critical to ever be connected to a network. Anesthesia equipment or surgical robots are two examples. Of course, the equipment vendor will tell you he has a "*magic box*" that cannot be hacked. **Don't believe it**. Anything can be hacked. Salesmen promise the Earth, Moon and Stars – but all they deliver is *rocks*.

Commercial organizations have been alarmed to discover through searches for internet-connected devices on **SHODAN, Censys** and **ZoomEye** that their BCS network is indeed accessible over the Internet – despite assurances to the contrary. Such a discovery counteracts the pervasive folk-myth of *security by obscurity* and even *air-gap* systems are vulnerable.

> **SHODAN -** *SHODAN* is a search engine that lets a user find specific types of computers (routers, servers, etc.) connected to the internet using a variety of filters. This can be information about the server software, what options the service supports, a welcome message or anything else that the client can find out before interacting with the server. *SHODAN* searches the Internet for publicly accessible devices, concentrating on *SCADA* systems. If your building control system is listed on *SHODAN*, it probably has been hacked. *SHODAN* will reveal a device's fingerprint, key exchange (kex) algorithms, server host key algorithms, encryption algorithms, MAC algorithms, and compression algorithms. One of the most popular searches is "*default password.*"

Again, one of the most popular searches is "*default password.*"

> **Censys** - *Censys* is a search engine designed to search for *internet-connected devices*. It collects data using both *ZMap* and *ZGrab* (an application layer scanner that operates via *ZMap*), which in this case scan the IPV4 address space. Censys can perform full-text searches. Here are two sample searches:
> https://www.censys.io/ipv4?q=80.http.get.status_code%3A%20200 – this allows you to search for all hosts with a specific *HTTP* status code. You can also just type in an IP address, such as: "66.24.206.155" or "71.20.34.200" (those are fake). To find hosts in 23.0.0.0/8 and 8.8.8.0/24, type in "23.0.0.0/8 or 8.8.8.0/24."

Once the *cracker* knows what software applications are running on the target network, he can develop a specific set of tools to *exploit known vulnerabilities*. For example, say the *cracker* learns the building controls system at a target data center is *Siemens* SIMATIC STEP 7 TIA (Portal). In February 2015, *Siemens* reported two vulnerabilities on that software. One vulnerability would allow a successful *man-in-the-middle attack* remotely. The other will allow a *cracker* with local access to reconstruct *protection-level passwords*. A *Siemens* software update is available but has not been installed at all data centers.

> **ZoomEye** - ZoomEye is a Chinese *search engine* similar to *SHODAN* that allows the user find specific network components. ZoomEye is *hacker-friendly* and uses *Xmap* and *Wmap* at its core for grabbing data from publicly exposed devices and web services (http://ics.zoomeye.org). ZoomEye allows you to search by:
>
> - **Application name and version** number
> - **Location**: **country** code (for example: UK, IT, ES, FR, CN, JP.) and name of **city**
> - **Port** number
> - **Name of the operating system** (for example os:linux)
> - **Service name**
> - **Hostname** (for example hostname:google.com)
> - **IP address** (for example ip:8.8.8.8)
> - **CIDR segment** (for example cidr:8.8.8.8/24)
> - **Domain name** (for example site:google.com)
> - **Headers** in HTTP request
> - **SEO keywords** defined inside <meta name="Keywords">
> - **Description** inside <meta name="description">
> - **Title** inside <title>
> - **Apache httpd** – finds results for *Apache* http servers
> - **device:"webcam"** – finds a list of webcams with an internet connection

Of course, if the building controls network is connected to the Internet, then the *cracker* can get in easily. I don't care how many assurances you get from equipment vendors that their "*magic box*" is impenetrable. *If your network is connected to the Internet, it can and <u>will</u> be hacked.* In fact, if it is connected to the Internet, I can say with confidence that it *has already been sniffed,* *hacked* and *mapped*. I would be surprised if you don't already have *spyware* and a number of *backdoors* already installed on your BCS network.

My recommendation is for you to bring in a third-party company to perform a **Penetration Test** and a **Vulnerability Test** to make sure your BCS is not connected to the Internet. *Do not rely on a vendor that sells you equipment for your BCS to pentest your network.* Hackers sometimes call these experts **Samurai.** That's *Hackerspeak* for a hacker who hires out for legal cracking jobs (an electronic locksmith). I highly recommend you have these tests performed frequently, and not necessarily advertise when the tests will be performed – even to your own line employees (more on that later).

A *penetration test* is a test performed by an *ethical hacker* to determine system vulnerability. *Pen-testing* is not the same as *vulnerability testing*. The intent of *vulnerability testing* is just to identify potential problems, but *pen-testing* is designed to *attack* those problems. The tools used for *pen-testing* can be classified into two kinds – *scanners* and *attackers*. This is because *pen-testing* is exploiting the weak spots. There are some software/tools that will only show you the weak spots, some that show *and* attack.

Making sure the BCS is not connected to the Internet may sound easy, but it isn't. Sometimes the BCS is designed to feed information to the company enterprise network. The problem is the enterprise network *is* connected to the Internet. An attacker that can hack into an enterprise network will use that as a gateway to hack into the BCS.

A good *Pentest* company such as ***FoxGuard Solutions***[2] will use a number of tools. **Nessus** is one of the most robust vulnerability identifier tools available. *Nessus* specializes in compliance checks, IP scans, sensitive data searches, and website scanning and aids in finding the 'weak-spots'. Another tool is **PunkSPIDER.** *PunkSPIDER* is a global web application vulnerability *search engine*. The driving force behind it is ***PunkSCAN***, a security scanner that can execute a massive number of security scans all at once. Among the types of attacks that *PunkSPIDER* can search for include *Cross-Site Scripting* (XSS), *Blind SQL Injection* (BSQLI), *Operating System Command Injection* (OSCI), and *Path Traversal* (TRAV).

Some equipment vendors will insist they need remote access to your BCS. Do not permit remote access to the BCS from *outside or inside* the building by anyone (maintain the air gap). This access is for *their convenience* and will degrade *your security*. Remember, if a device has an IP Address – it can be hacked. It's bad enough that all your BCS networks have already been mapped by *crackers*, let's not make it easy for them to get in.

---

[2] Full Disclosure: FoxGuard Solutions is one of my clients, so I know they are good.

Disable Everything You Don't Need

When purchasing new BCS equipment, include language in the Request for Proposal (RFP) requiring the vendor to remove all unnecessary software, disable unused ports and install the latest software patches before you accept the work and that new patches/fixes are implemented when they are released. The vendor must certify in writing that the equipment complies with all the requirements in the RFP – regardless whatever weasel words they sneak into their proposal.

Require the vendor to change all default passwords and set appropriately secure login credentials. Do not purchase equipment with hard-wired default passwords that YOU cannot change. The most common configuration problem is credentials management (i.e., weak passwords, shared user accounts and insufficiently protected credentials), followed by weak or non-existent firewall rules and network design weaknesses.

Control access to trusted devices. For example, for access to a segmented network, use a bastion host with access control lists (ACLs) for ingress/egress access. Never place a computer or a monitor where they can be seen by outsiders (such as facing a window) where a specially-designed aerial hacker drone can monitor the network such as a **scanner hack**.

> **Scanner Hack** - Researchers in Israel have shown off a novel technique that would allow attackers to wirelessly command devices using a laser light, bypassing so-called *air gaps*. Firewalls and *intrusion detection systems* can block communication going to and from suspicious domains and IP addresses over the Internet. To bypass normal detection methods, researchers in Israel were able to use a **laser-equipped aerial drone** to communicate covertly with *malware*. The technique uses a **flatbed scanner** as the gateway through which an attacker can send commands to their malware on a victim's network. The attack would also work by hijacking an existing light source installed near the scanner, such as a "smart" lightbulb. The attack could be used against industrial control systems to shut down processes on "air gapped" networks, which aren't directly connected to the internet.

In order to reduce the number of threat vectors, you should remove or disable any unnecessary applications or capabilities. Better to remove than disable something that can later be enabled without your knowledge. Disable unused ports as well as remote protocols that are insecure (like Telnet). Disable all protocols that communicate inbound to your trusted resources that are not critical to functionality.

Maintain the *air-gap* of your BCS networks at all costs. **Air Gap** computers are physically isolated from unsecured computer networks, such as the public Internet or an unsecured local area network for security purposes. Air gap computers are not connected by wire or wirelessly and (generally) cannot communicate directly with each other. Rely on the **Ten-Finger Interface**.

> **Ten-Finger Interface** - *Hackerspeak* referring to the air gap between two networks that cannot be directly connected for security reasons; interface is achieved by placing two terminals side by side and having an operator read from one and type into the other.

eMail is the *cracker*'s preferred method of gaining access to any network that has Internet access. **NEVER** allow email access on the **Process Network or the Control Network**. Employees should have a separate computer for email, preferably not in the same room as the BCS servers. Don't even install *Microsoft Office* on BCS workstations. The *process network* usually hosts the *SCADA* servers and *human-machine interfaces*. The *control network* hosts all the devices on one side that controls the actuators and sensors of the physical layer, and on the other side provide the control interface to the *process network*.

Financially-motivated *cyber-criminals* are now launching tailored, victim-specific *spear-phishing* campaigns. These *crackers* are targeting a large number of organizations and they quickly shift *tools, tactics, and procedures* (TTPs). In years past, cyber-crime was frequently opportunistic. Today, *cyber-criminals* are exhibiting unusual persistence using tools developed by *advanced persistent threat* (APT) actors and are attempting to re-compromise an organization after remediation.

A *cracker* typically will send an email containing *Active Content* (carries out or triggers actions automatically without the intervention of a user) such as a *Remote Access Trojan* (RAT) to an employee such as a building maintenance technician. I suggest you provide basic personal *cyber-hygiene training* to the entire workforce. I guarantee that will prevent most cyber-attacks because **91%** of successful data breaches started with a *spear-phishing attack*.

Also, do not enable web surfing from workstations on critical networks. If you already disconnected critical networks from the Internet, that is not a problem, I'm just saying. Perhaps, install one Internet-connected computer as **a kiosk** where employees can check email or surf the web. Heck, everybody has a smart phone anyway, so they don't need to access the Internet on their desktop computer.

If the only thing you get out of this is to **separate email traffic and web surfing from critical networks**, I will be happy.

Another thing, when you buy new equipment and remove a computer or server from your network, take out the hard drives and have them chopped up. Even erasing the data with a large magnet is not enough to ensure someone cannot retrieve the data once it's out of your hands.

I included some basic **Cyber-Hygiene** for email and USB stick **Do's and Don't**s in my book *"Cybersecurity for Hospitals and Healthcare Facilities."* That book also includes tips on creating strong passwords as well as example phishing text used by *crackers.* (Do you really think somebody in Africa is gonna wire you some money if you click on that attachment?)

Eliminate Common BCS Vulnerabilities

Key automation and control devices should be grouped into zones that share common security-level requirements. Utilize network segmentation to secure resources like VES systems, ICS, and devices. If you must have some connectivity, install a **DMZ**. If it were me, however, I wouldn't even trust that.

> **Demilitarized Zone (DMZ)** - An interface on a routing firewall that is similar to the interfaces found on the firewall's protected side. Traffic moving between the DMZ and other interfaces on the protected side of the firewall still goes through the firewall and can have firewall protection policies applied. It is a physical or logical subnetwork that contains and exposes the external-facing services (email, Web and Domain Name System servers) to an untrusted network. And, as far as I am concerned, all outside networks are untrusted.

Require user name/password combinations for all systems, including those that are not deemed "trustworthy." At a minimum, require vendor implement two-factor authentication on all trusted systems for any user account. If it were me, I would implement **3 Level Password Protection.** Requiring an additional password to authorize critical operations greatly reduces the surface area to attack the secondary credentials since they are used less often. For example: a *power-on* password, a *parameter setting* password, and a *parameter correction* password. Requiring re-authentication to perform special actions can protect against **Cross-Site Request Forgery** (CSRF) attacks. CSRF is also known as *one-click attack* or *session riding.*

I recommend you change passwords frequently, and sometimes with no-notice. Do not rely on employees to develop passwords because password attack software takes advantage of the fact that people tend to use uppercase characters at the start of passwords and numbers at the end. I recommend use of an **Automated Password Generator.** This uses an algorithm which creates random passwords that have no association with a particular user. It is also more effective against a **Dictionary Attack** and a **Brute Force Attack**.

Be on the lookout for a misconfigured and unencrypted router, which could potentially provide a gateway for *crackers.* Also, don't use a weak and outmoded form of encryption such as *WEP.*

I recommend you collect and aggregate the data related to login failures from all the hosts to check for *doorknob-rattling*. A **Doorknob-Rattling Attack** is when a *cracker* attempts a very few common username and password combinations on several computers resulting in very few failed login attempts.

> **Dictionary Attack** - A dictionary attack takes place when an attacker utilizes a dictionary in an attempt to crack a password. Essentially, words from the dictionary are inputted into the password field to try to guess the password. Programs and tools exist that allow hackers to easily try various combinations of words in the dictionary against a user's password.

A robust password management system is not enough for critical systems. Here, I recommend **Multi-Factor Authentication**. This is a method of computer access control in which a user is granted access only after successfully presenting several separate pieces of evidence to an authentication mechanism – typically at least two of the following categories: knowledge (password you know), possession (something you have), and biometrics (who you are). **Two-Factor Authentication** (also known as **2FA**) is a combination of *two* different components.

A word of caution about two-factor authentication when an SMS message is sent to a smart phone. NIST is no longer recommending solutions that use SMS because they may be vulnerable to **SS7 Cyber-Attacks**. SS7 (Signaling System 7) is a set of telephony signaling protocols used for data-roaming with vulnerabilities that allow attackers to listen to calls, intercept text messages, and pinpoint a device's location armed with just the target's phone number. Anyone can purchase SS7 access and send a routing request to direct a target's SMS-based text messages to another device, and, in the case of the bank accounts, steal any codes needed to login or greenlight money transfers (after the hackers obtained victim passwords).

> **Brute-Force Attack** - This type of cyber-attack is typically used as an end-all method to crack a difficult password. A brute-force attack is executed when an attacker tries to use all possible combinations of letters, numbers, and symbols to enter a correct password. Programs exist that help a *cracker* achieve this, such as **Zip Password Cracker Pro**. Any password can be cracked using the brute-force method, but it can take a very long time. The longer and more intricate a password is, the longer it will take a computer to try all of the possible combinations. **Cain & Abel** is a tool for cracking **encrypted passwords** or network keys.

I would also be leery of **One-Time Passwords.** A one-time password is a code issued by a small electronic device every 30 or 60 seconds that is valid for only one login session or transaction. Online thieves have created real-time *Trojan horse* programs that can issue transactions to a bank while the account holder is online, turning the one-time password into *a huge vulnerability*.

You may want to consider **Time-Dependent Passwords**. These are passwords that are valid only at a certain time of day or during a specified interval of time. The password for someone who normally works days would not work after hours, and vice versa. This would also help defend against a **Verifier Impersonation Attack**. This is an attack where the attacker impersonates the verifier in an authentication protocol, and somehow obtains another user's password (for example by **Shoulder Surfing**).

I recommend using a **Shadow Password File.** This is a building control system file in which encrypted user passwords are stored so that they aren't available to people who try to break into the building controls system. Also, make sure you keep **Escrow Passwords** in a *locked* safe. These are passwords that are written down and stored in a secure location that are used by emergency personnel when privileged personnel are unavailable.

Never store passwords in the open (unencrypted). Some searches on **GoogleDiggity** (a traditional Google hacking tool) can even retrieve the username and password list from *Microsoft FrontPage* servers.

Whenever possible, use **application layer encryption** (to avoid sensitive information being logged), end-to-end encryption, and encrypt files stored on hosts and servers. Network activity logs should always be encrypted. SSL is neither a network layer protocol nor an application layer protocol. It is one that "sits" between both layers.

Use real-time *anti-malware* protection and real-time *network scanning* locally on trusted hosts and where applicable. Rely on **Real-Time Protection** that immediately detects malware before it can do any harm by blocking or suspending malicious processes and infected files that try to start or connect to your system, effectively preventing malware from damaging your network and files. Use real-time registry protection to detect attempted registry changes. Use a program that alerts you when a program tries to make changes to your *registry*.

Develop a threat modeling system. Understand who's attacking you and why. There is a big difference between the ability of a garden-variety *script kiddie* and a *state-sponsored* organization bent on interfering with critical infrastructure. Designing an attack scenario to exploit a particular physical process requires a solid engineering background and in-depth *destructive* knowledge of the target SCADA system (**Cyber-Physical Attack Engineering**). Hacking a chemical plant, for example, requires knowledge of physics, chemistry and engineering, as well as a great deal about how the network is laid out, and a keen understanding of process-aware defensive systems. This represents a high (but not insurmountable) barrier to entry to garden-variety *script kiddies*, but is not a major obstacle for a *foreign intelligence service*.

Your company or utility may be a purely commercial enterprise, but be advised that military installations rely on public utilities, just like everyone else. All victims are not necessarily the targets. An attack on a company that provides vital utilities will be targeted in time of **Cyberwar.** These are actions by a nation-state to penetrate another nation's computers or networks for the purposes of causing damage or disruption. *Cyberwarfare* involves the use and targeting of computers and networks in warfare between nations or non-state actors, such as terrorist groups, political or ideological extremist groups, hacktivists, and transnational criminal organizations.

Keep in mind that *Foreign Policy Magazine* puts the size of China's "*hacker army*" at anywhere from 50,000 to 100,000 individuals. Although to date cyberwarfare has been limited to attacking information and communications networks, the possibility exists for cyber-attacks against computer-controlled equipment capable of causing harm and even death to a nation's civilian population.

Monitor All Activity on the BCS Network on a 24-hour Basis.

Inventory all direct and indirect trusts and associations (e.g., personnel, vendors, contractors, supply chain partners). This can be done by monitoring access (including physical access, when relevant) over time. Pay particular attention to those with too much privilege such as administrators, who should not have super access to the entire system contents or use shared passwords.

Improve logging in on trusted environments in addition to passing logs to *Security Information and Event Management* (SIEM) devices for third-party backup/analysis. Monitor systems and networks users are accessing over time for typical behavioral information between these trusts, their applications and their traffic. Assess and inventory all access to networks, systems and specific resources.

The system health of each cyber asset should be monitored for suspected system use of memory, CPU and number of network connections. Perform unscheduled, no-notice exercises to test network vulnerability to cyber-physical attack. Perform a periodic sweep (unannounced) of the area looking for **Rogue Access Points** and **Hidden Private Networks**.

> **Rogue Access Point -** A rogue access point is a wireless access point that has been installed on a secure network without explicit authorization from a local network administrator, whether added by a well-meaning employee or by a malicious insider. Although it is technically easy for a well-meaning employee to install a "*soft access point*" or an inexpensive wireless router - perhaps to make access from mobile devices easier - it is likely that they will configure this as "open", or with poor security, and potentially allow access to unauthorized parties. If an attacker installs a rogue access point they are able to run various types of vulnerability scanners, and rather than having to be physically inside the building, a *cracker* can attack remotely - perhaps from a reception area, adjacent building, or car parking lot.

Snort is a network intrusion detection system that can detect probes or attacks and stealth port scans. A **stealth port scan** is designed to probe a server or host for *open ports* without being detected. The purpose is to identify services running on a host and exploit vulnerabilities.

> **Hidden Private Networks** can bypass the corporate network security. A computer that is being spied upon can be plugged into a legitimate corporate network that is heavy monitored for malware activity and at same time belongs to a private Wi-Fi network outside of the company network that is leaking confidential information off of an employee's computer. A computer like this is easily set up by a *double-agent* working in the IT department by installing a second wireless card in a computer. Using special software, he can remotely monitor an employee's computer through this second interface card without them being aware of a *side-band communication* channel pulling information off of his computer.

Use *intrusion detection* methods to look for attack signatures or anomalies that indicate a network attack may be in progress or may have already occurred. Use intrusion detection tools to *monitor transactions* at the *network layer* based on the source and destination addresses and protocol types and can look for "signatures" of known attack scenarios and anomalous behavioral patterns. Implement **Continuous Diagnostics and Mitigation (CDM).**

> **Continuous Diagnostics and Mitigation** is a dynamic approach to fortifying the cybersecurity of government networks and systems. CDM provides federal agencies with capabilities and tools that identify cybersecurity risks on an ongoing basis, prioritize these risks based upon potential impacts, and enable cybersecurity personnel to mitigate the most significant problems first. Agency-installed network sensors perform an automated search for known cyber flaws. Results feed into a local dashboard that produces customized reports, alerting network managers to their worst and most critical cyber risks based on standardized and weighted risk scores. Prioritized alerts enable agencies to efficiently allocate resources based on the severity of the risk. Progress reports track results, which can be used to compare security posture among department/agency networks. Summary information can feed into an enterprise-level dashboard to inform and situational awareness into cybersecurity risk posture across the federal government.

Scan the Wi-Fi spectrum at your data center frequently looking for weak and open Wi-Fi networks, wireless printers without passwords, servers with outdated and vulnerable software, and unencrypted login pages to back-end databases. These are serious cyber-attack threat vectors.

Use network vulnerability scanners to assess the configuration of the BCS network, identify security deficiencies and recommend countermeasures.

Apply a *digital signature* to individual or combinations of event logs with sequence numbers to ensure that the event logs are complete.

Use sophisticated tools to automatically scan large amounts of data to analyze *event logs* and to present *suspicious events* to the auditor in a user-friendly manner.

Set up **Honeypots** and **Canaries**. These are "traps" to alert you when *crackers* are lurking in the shadows trying to hack your equipment. You can program setpoint traps, such as a specific temperature range for a certain area, to restrict override changes from going outside of set parameters and include PIN control on user access to system changes. You can also use a timed feature, to automatically revert to original settings after a temporary override period.

> **Honeypot** - A system (e.g., a Web server) or system resource (e.g., a file on a server) that is designed to be attractive to potential *crackers* and intruders and has no authorized users other than its administrators.
>
> **Canary** - Anything that can send up an observable alert if something happens. For example: you can set up a computer on a subnet such that no other computer should ever access that. If something touches it, you know it's outside normal behavior. Also, called a *tripwire*.

Set up a **Continuous Diagnostics and Mitigation (CDM)** program. This is a dynamic approach to fortifying the cybersecurity of BCS networks. CDM provides users with capabilities and tools that identify cybersecurity risks on an ongoing basis, prioritize these risks based upon potential impacts, and enable cybersecurity personnel to mitigate the most significant problems first. Network sensors perform an automated search for known cyber flaws. Results feed into a local dashboard that produces customized reports, alerting network managers to their worst and most critical cyber risks based on standardized and weighted risk scores. Prioritized alerts enable agencies to efficiently allocate resources based on the severity of the risk. Progress reports track results, which can be used to compare security posture among department networks. Summary information can feed into an enterprise-level dashboard to inform and situational awareness into cybersecurity risk posture across the data center.

When all else fails, set up a **Cyber Recovery Plan** that provides guidance to building maintenance personnel when responding to an intentional cyber-attack on a BCS. The Plan instructs personnel on documenting the nature and scope of the cyber-attack and instructs the **Incident Response Team** how to restore normal building operations without triggering further damage.

A **Cyber Booby Trap** is when an attacker embeds malware in the building controls system designed to be triggered by actions of the building maintenance staff. For example: the initial indication of a cyber-physical attack may be that the cracker turned off the water to a boiler. The maintenance personnel in the control room are unaware that the malware also pumped all the water out of the boiler and turned up the heat. Once the boiler is superheated, the action of turning on the water triggers an explosion. The cracker needed the triggering action by building maintenance personnel to initiate the damage. Before turning the water back on, maintenance personnel should make sure the power to the boiler is not turned on by manually checking the boiler and NOT rely on the BCS that has probably been rendered unreliable by the cracker. Also, the boiler should be purged before it comes back on line.

Monitor Insider (and Outsider) Behavior for Anomalies

Maintain workforce situational awareness and be on the lookout for **Insider Threats** such as counterproductive work behavior. This is defined as intentional behaviors that are contrary to legitimate organizational interests, including sabotage and espionage. The CERT Insider Threat Center includes a database of more than 850 cases of insider threats, including instances of fraud, theft and sabotage. Keep in mind that current access control systems that are designed to prevent the outsider threat.

> **Insider Threats** - Insider threat to a data center's critical infrastructure is more serious than outsider threats because an outside attacker is less likely to know the BCS network vulnerabilities and its weaknesses as well as an insider would. The behavioral characteristics of employees are potential indicators and patterns to detect insider threat activity. No one behavior by itself would be an issue, but questionable behaviors are more likely to be manifested in *multiple observables*.

Watch for personal predispositions and stressors such as serious divorce, personal financial problems, mental health disorders, personality problems, social skills and decision-making biases, and *a history of rule conflicts* as *precursors of malicious events*. A financial sector report released in 2012 noted that 80% of the malicious acts were committed at work during working hours; 81% of the perpetrators planned their actions beforehand; 33% were described as "difficult" and 17% as being "disgruntled". Financial gain was a motive in 81% of cases, revenge in 23% of cases, and 27% of the people carrying out malicious acts were in financial difficulties at the time.

Avoid over-dependence on any insider (two-man rule). Address counterproductive work behavior consistently and fairly. Perceived variations in justice is a potential employee stressor. Perceived injustice is the most common cause of sabotage. **Do not ignore security policy rule violations.** Enforce limits on access and hold individuals accountable for their actions.

Monitoring insider behavior is particularly important when organization changes occur such as changes in management, organizational sanctions, or negative-workplace events (e.g., pay cut, missed promotion, below-average performance appraisal). Question anomalous behavior (why is insider working outside of normal working hours?). Watch for an insider **Tipping Point** (the *first observed event* at which an insider became disgruntled such as insider demoted, reprimanded for harassing coworker, or is being fired).

Insiders typically commit malicious acts *within 7 days of a tipping point*.
Review the audit logs for actions or accesses that seem inappropriate. Reviews should be more frequent and extensive for individuals with higher privileges.

How Much Damage Can an Insider Do?

Recently, a former contract security guard at a California company was found guilty of hacking his former employer, stealing proprietary software, and trashing the company network two weeks after he resigned his job. He had used an admin password to log into the company's payroll program and tampered with his overtime hours and work records. He gained access to the firm's network and stole archived emails, accounting software, and the databases used for accounting, invoices, and payroll operations. He also deleted or corrupted backup files and started the process of reformatting the company's various drives when the intrusion was discovered and the servers disconnected from the internet.

Critical vendor partners should be monitored for new business relationships, financial results, organizational changes and governmental associations. All external supplier companies and consultant firms should be monitored and include content analysis of social media (e.g., *LinkedIn, Facebook, Twitter,* and *Youtube*) using tools such as *Maltego* and **content scraping** and search engines like *Devon Technologies*.

Monitor the Building Equipment Looking for Anomalies

It is probably easier to detect a cyber-physical attack (when it occurs) by looking at how the equipment is operating than it is to detect subtle software anomalies or dropped packets. Although boiler water temperature and pressure rising dangerous levels doesn't necessarily signal that a cyber-physical attack is underway, it could be an attack. Don't assume it isn't a cyber-attack out of hand. Look for signs that the controls have been manipulated. Compare what the computer *says* is happening with what the equipment is actually doing. Remember, a sneaky attacker will change the *setpoints* higher than normal so the computer will not *know* something is wrong.

Malicious attackers are more likely to use the process control systems to make equipment "*misbehave*" while appearing to operate normally. At the Iranian nuclear plant, *Stuxnet* manipulated the *calibration systems* so the plant workers didn't see the real pressure readings that would have flagged the problems with the devices early on. Had the workers manually checked the equipment itself frequently, they would have noticed the discrepancy.

A malicious attacker would schedule his attack when it would be *less likely to be detected* or when it could *do the most damage. Startup and shutdown* of a process plant are the two most dangerous operational modes of the plant. A well-qualified attacker would know the planned startup sequence of operations and manipulate the amount of heat or the flow of fluids to corrupt *the process* and damage *the hardware*.

For example, industrial distillation is typically performed in large, vertical cylindrical columns known as *distillation towers* or *distillation columns*. The amount of heat entering a distillation column is a crucial operating parameter, addition of *excess or insufficient heat* to the column can lead to *foaming, weeping, entrainment*, or *flooding*. If the column contains liquid during *pressuring*, excessive vapor flows will cause *flooding* and *gas lifting of the liquid*, resulting in liquid discharge into the *relief header* and damage the column internals.

Cyber-Attacks on Building Controls

Aurora Vulnerability Cyber-Physical Attack - In 2007, the Idaho National Laboratory (INL) conducted a test to demonstrate how a cyber-physical attack could destroy physical components of the electric grid. INL used a computer program to rapidly open and close a diesel generator's circuit breakers out of phase from the rest of the grid. Every time the breakers were closed, the torque from the synchronization caused the generator to bounce and shake, eventually causing parts of the generator to be ripped apart and sent flying as far as 80 feet. This vulnerability can be mitigated by preventing out-of-phase opening and closing of the circuit breakers. A cyber-physical attack that takes down the commercial power grid will cause a rise in mortality rates as health and safety systems fail, a drop in trade as ports shut down, and disruption to transport and infrastructure.

Basin Heater Cyber-Physical Attack - An electric immersion heater is installed in *a cooling tower* to prevent the cold-water basin from completely freezing over during shutdown or standby. It is NOT designed to prevent icing during operation. A cracker can cause the cooling tower to freeze up in Winter by shutting down the unit or cutting power to the basin heater. A cracker can also turn the basin heater on in Summer to reduce the efficiency of the unit and run up energy costs.

Auto-Hacking Attack - An easy-to-use device with the auto-hacking function will hack into a Wi-Fi network without a computer. Simply turn on the device, select a network and the device will hack it automatically. It is a standalone machine and does not require boot from disc or computer.

Computerized Maintenance Management System (CMMS) Cyber-Attack - Unfortunately, a CMMS depends heavily on connectivity to the Internet as well as wireless communications to work efficiently. Building maintenance personnel are notified by the CMMS when equipment needs attention such as when a pump or valve malfunctions by generating and sending a work order to a mobile device. Personnel can access information wirelessly such as past maintenance history, preventive maintenance performed, all the specifications for the device including capacity, normal operating parameters and even whether spare parts are on hand and where they are located in the storage room. Some CMMS databases include tenant information such as who requested maintenance, the room number and telephone number. Some databases contain information such as security clearance for staff, labor rates, vacation schedule and contact information. The CMMS would be a great tool to target maintenance personnel for spear phishing attacks.

When a cracker breaks into the CMMS, he can see a great deal of information about the building and how it is operated. A cracker can see which pieces of equipment are high-priority assets, which can be considered safety hazards and the trigger points for failure alarms and automatic shutdown. A cracker can see whether spare parts are on hand so he can target equipment that would take longer to repair. Another thing to consider is that the CMMS is typically tied directly to the BCS network making the CMMS a possible attack vector for crackers.

Cyber-Drone - A cyber-drone can carry lightweight but powerful hacking platforms like Wi-Fi Pineapple and Raspberry Pi, packaged with an external battery pack and cellular connection, for powerful eavesdropping and man-in-the-middle attacks. A cyber-drone (or a swarm) can search for Wi-Fi wireless networks connected to a BCS at a facility and hack into networks when they are found. A cyber-drone can fly outside a skyscraper and find vulnerable networks with minimal interference. For example, a cyber-drone can land on a roof and target wireless printers because they often are the weak link in a company's wireless network. Wireless printers are typically supplied with the Wi-Fi connection open by default, and many companies forget to close this hole when they add the device to their Wi-Fi networks. This open connection potentially provides an access point for outsiders to connect to a BCS network. It is also possible for a cyber-drone to shut down computer systems and other nearby electronic systems from the sky through targeted emission of microwaves.

Anti-drone technology is beginning to come on the market for WLAN customers as cyber-drones become attached to more verified network attacks. Fluke Networks has released the first cyber-drone detection signature as an update to its AirMagnet Enterprise wireless IDS/IPS product that alerts customers to drone-specific signals. Cyber-drones are controlled via an ad hoc network and AirMagnet can detect the command-and-control signaling. The AirMagnet also can detect video transmission streams. Once alerted, the network administrator can either attempt to locate the drone and its operator or take RF or WLAN system-level countermeasures.

Cyborg Unplug is a plug-and-play network appliance that may be useful against cyber-drones. It automatically detects and disconnects a range of Internet-connected surveillance devices including Dropcam, Google Glass and Wi-Fi-enabled drones by breaking uploads and streams. It sniffs the air for wireless signatures from devices known to pose a risk to personal privacy, Cyborg Unplug will disconnect them, stopping them from streaming video, audio and data to the Internet and it sends an email alert. Most wireless devices used for surveillance; stream data to a machine on the Internet or in a nearby room allowing for remote surveillance while ensuring the offending device contains no evidence (files) of the abuse.

Jamming Attack - An attack in which a device is used to emit electromagnetic energy on a wireless network's frequency to make it unusable. SOURCE: SP 800-48

Keystroke Injection Attack - A USB thumb drive (called a "Rubber Ducky") containing malware that fools a computer into thinking it is a keyboard. Whether it be a Windows, Mac, Linux or Android device, any USB device claiming to be a Keyboard HID (Human Input Device) will be automatically detected and accepted by most modern operating systems. By taking advantage of this inherent trust with scripted keystrokes at speeds beyond 1,000 words per minute traditional countermeasures can be bypassed. A cracker will change the VID/PID on a thumb drive to fool the computer into thinking it is another device, with the intent to load malicious payload, either a file or scripted code. This is very effective because most anti-virus software is looking at files, not scripted language entered by keyboard.

Parasitic Wi-Fi - It is possible to induce parasitic signals on the audio front end of voice-command-capable devices such as the iPhone. A cracker can send radio waves to any Android or iPhone that has Google Now or Siri enabled. The hack uses the phone's headphone cord as an antenna to convert electrical signals that appear to the phone's operating system to be audio coming from the microphone. Anything you can do through the voice interface you cn do remotely and discretely through electromagnetic waves.

Power over Ethernet (PoE) Hack - Technology that uses unused conductors on Ethernet cabling to power low voltage devices. Up to 44 volts 350 ma is available. POE Plus can provide up to 25.5 Watts. An attacker that hacks into a security network and causes a power surge on the Ethernet cabling may be able to cause devices to fail.

Probing Attack - To attempt to connect to well-known services which may be running on a system; done to see if the system exists, and potentially to identify the software it is running.

Reflected File Download Attack (RFD) - RFD is a web attack vector that enables attackers to gain complete control over a victim's machine by forcing the browser to initiate a file download from a trusted domain using a Windows security features bypass. Once inside the user's computer, the attacker can use PowerShell to download additional payload and acquire admin rights. This attack completely disables all warnings and files execute immediately. See Google Chrome Attacks.

Remote Access Tool (RAT) - A piece of software that allows a remote "operator" to control a system as if he has physical access to that system. While desktop sharing and remote administration have many legal uses, "RAT" software is usually associated with criminal or malicious activity. Malicious RAT software is typically installed without the victim's knowledge, often as payload of a Trojan horse, and will try to hide its operation from the victim and from security software. Such tools provide an operator the following capabilities:
- Screen/camera capture or image control
- File management (download/upload/execute/etc.)
- Shell control (from command prompt)
- Computer control (power off/on/log off if remote feature is supported)
- Registry management (query/add/delete/modify)
- Hardware Destroyer (overclocker)

Remote-to-Local User (R2L) Attack - A remote-to-local cyber-attack occurs when a cracker who has the ability to send packets over a network (but who does not have a valid user account on the building automation system) exploits a system vulnerability to gain access as a user.

Rogue Access Point - A rogue access point is a wireless access point that has been installed on a secure network without explicit authorization from a local network administrator, whether added by a well-meaning employee or by a malicious attacker. Although it is technically easy for a well-meaning employee to install a "soft access point" or an inexpensive wireless router - perhaps to make access from mobile devices easier - it is likely that they will configure this as "open", or with poor security, and potentially allow access to unauthorized parties. If an attacker installs an access point they are able to run various types of vulnerability scanners, and rather than having to be physically inside the organization, can attack remotely - perhaps from a reception area, adjacent building, or car parking lot.

Social Engineering Attack - Social engineering is the art and science of getting people to do something you want them to do that they might not do in the normal course of action. Instead of collecting information by technical means, intruders might also apply methods of social engineering such as impersonating individuals on the telephone, or using other persuasive means (e.g., tricking, convincing, inducing, enticing, provoking) to encourage someone to disclose information. Attackers look for information about who the target does business with, both suppliers and customers and they are particularly interested in IT support. They gather this information to better understand roles and responsibilities. They use this information to pose as someone from one of these companies. Attackers look for information such as birthdays, who was recently promoted or who just had a baby. Hackers do not discount any information they uncover. They will use bad relationships between IT department and other offices as a wedge to gain information.

Soft Access Point (Soft AP) - A soft access point can be set up on a Wi-Fi adapter without the need of a physical Wi-Fi router. With Windows 7 virtual Wi-Fi capabilities and Intel My Wi-Fi technology, one can easily set up a Soft AP on their machine. Once up and running, one can share the network access available on a machine to other Wi-Fi users that will connect to the soft AP. If any employee sets up a Soft AP on their machine inside the corporate premises and shares the corporate network through it, then this Soft AP behaves as Rogue Access Point.

Thermostat Hacks - Intelligent thermostats can track a user's heat and air-conditioning habits, learn user preferences, and generally surveil a location remotely. One HVAC controls manufacturer has programmed their thermostats to report temperature settings over the Internet to a company database every 12 seconds. In addition, there has been at least one instance where a thermostat produced in the Far East was manufactured so it was retasked remotely (over the Internet) to eavesdrop on sensitive conversations in a conference room.

Vampire Tap - A device for physically connecting a station (e.g. a computer or printer) to a network that uses 10BASE5 cabling. This device clamps onto and "bites" into the cable (hence the vampire name), forcing a spike through a hole drilled through the outer shielding to contact the inner conductor while other spikes bite into the outer conductor. Vampire taps allow new connections to be made on a given physical cable while the cable is in use. Also, called a piercing tap.

Wireless Sensor Network (WSN) Attack - These cyber-attacks prevent sensors from detecting and transmitting data through the building automation network infrastructure.

Preserving Forensic Data

Following are digital forensics recommendations from ICS-CERT.

Preserving forensic data is an essential aspect of any incident response plan. The forensic data acquired during the overall incident response process are critical to containing the current intrusion and improving security to defend against the next attack. An organization's network defenders should make note of the following recommendations for retention of essential forensic data:

- Keep detailed notes of all observations, including dates/times, mitigation steps taken/not taken, device logging enabled/disabled, and machine names for suspected compromised equipment. More information is generally better than less information.
- When possible, capture live system data (i.e., current network connections and open processes) prior to disconnecting a compromised machine from the network.
- Capture a forensic image of the system memory prior to powering down the system.
- When powering down a system, physically pull the plug from the wall rather than gracefully shutting down. Forensic data can be destroyed if the operating system (OS) executes a normal shut down process.
- After shutting down, capture forensic images of the host hard drives.
- Avoid running any antivirus software "after the fact" as the antivirus scan changes critical file dates and impedes discovery and analysis of suspected malicious files and timelines.
- Avoid making any changes to the OS or hardware, including updates and patches, as they might overwrite important information relevant to the analysis. Organizations should consult with trained forensic investigators for advice and assistance prior to implementing any recovery or forensic efforts.

When a compromised host is identified, it should be disconnected from the network for forensic data collection (but not powered off, as noted above). When all available data have been retained from the infected host, the organization should follow established internal policies for recovering the host.

What to do When the Shit Hits the Fan Coil Unit

Of course, building engineers assume a cyber-physical attack can't happen because of safety devices installed to prevent catastrophic events. It's true that many building control systems have hard-wired safeties designed to shut down equipment and these hard-wired safeties typically are not controlled by the BCS. However, *an attacker can use these safety devices as part of the attack* – in fact, the hacker may be *counting on safety devices turning things off*. Keep in mind that the Chernobyl nuclear plant also had safety devices – that were turned off – by insiders.

Accept the fact that eventually your data center equipment will be the target of a cyber-physical attack. The only choices you have in this matter are *how* your building will be attacked (by reducing the number of possible attack vectors), how you will *respond* to an attack, and how you plan to *recover* from an attack.

My book on *Cyber-Physical Attack Recovery Procedures* explains in greater detail how to determine if a cyber-physical attack on a building is underway and how to mitigate the event, so I won't go into that here. For more detailed information on Recovery Procedures Plans and a template to prepare your own custom plan, see my other book titled, *"Cyber-Physical Attack Recovery Procedures."*

When a cyber-physical attack occurs, the last thing you want to do is *make things up as you go*. The time to figure out what must be done when an attack happens is not during a crisis. Decide NOW the actions that need to be taken when you first detect a cyber-physical attack so you can make decisions quickly and take proper action to mitigate the impact of the attack. Prepare a written, customized **Recovery Procedures Plan** that includes detailed responsibilities and specific tasks for emergency response activities and building resumption operations based upon pre-defined time frames. Your employees should know how to react when a building is attacked.

For strategies for **forensic evidence of a cyber-physical attack**, see another of my books titled, *"Cybersecurity for Hospitals and Healthcare Facilities."*

Key Takeaways

1. Patching a server could disrupt the BCS software so they are often unpatched resulting in vulnerabilities remaining that would normally be patched. Install software **patches** as soon as they are released and keep a log.
2. Make frequent **backups** of important files.
3. BCS's are often installed without the IT department's knowledge.
4. IT staff is unfamiliar with BCS's and they don't know if the connection to a port is normal, so it is often ignored.
5. The only reason a BCS should be connected to the Internet is when you are *trying* to be hacked and you *want* to experience a cyber-physical attack.
6. Be ready to go completely off the grid at a moments notice.

6. ELECTROMAGNETIC INTERFERENCE

Transient Voltages

Before talking about electromagnetic interference (EMI), we need to look at how changes in voltage can harm the data center building's electrical equipment. Transients are momentary changes in voltage or current that occur over a short period of time. Also, called surges or spikes. Transients are divided into two categories which are easy to identify: impulsive and oscillatory. An impulsive low-frequency transient rises in 0.1 ms and lasts more than 1 ms. A medium-frequency impulsive transient lasting between 50 ns to 1 ms and oscillatory transients between 5 and 500 kHz are less frequent than the low-frequency types but have much higher amplitude. These transients may not propagate as easily as the low-frequency types but may cause arcing faults on the power distribution system which result in voltage sag on many power systems. The vast majority of transients are produced within the facility due to device switching, static discharge, and arcing. The inductive "kick" from a 5-horsepower motor turning on can produce a transient in excess of 1,000 volts. A motor with a faulty winding, commutator, or other insulation faults can produce a continuous stream of transients exceeding 600 volts! Even transformers can produce a large transient, particularly when energizing. Arcing can generate transients from faulty contacts in breakers, switches, and contactors when voltage jumps the gap. When this gap is "jumped" the voltage rises suddenly and the most common effect is an oscillatory-ring-type transient. Faulty connections and grounds can produce arcing.

Transients cause electronic devices to operate erratically. Equipment could lock up or produce garbled results. These types of disruptions may be difficult to diagnose because faulty transient voltage surge suppression equipment can actually INCREASE the incidents of failure. Integrated circuits may fail immediately. Transients cause motors to run at higher temperatures and interrupt the normal timing of the motor and result in "micro-jogging". This type of disruption produces motor vibration, noise, and excessive heat. Transient activity causes early failure of all types of lights. The building's electrical distribution system is also affected by degrading the contacting surfaces of switches, disconnects, and circuit breakers. Intense transient activity can produce "nuisance tripping" of breakers by heating the breaker and "fooling" it into reacting to a non-existent current demand. This type of activity can be induced by a well-planned cyber-physical attack.

Intentional Electromagnetic Interference (IEMI)

Disruptive and data altering electromagnetic signals caused by the malicious use of electromagnetic weapons (non-detonation, within targeted footprints).

Geomagnetic Storm (GS)

A geomagnetic storm is (completely distinct from EMP) a temporary disturbance of the Earth's magnetosphere caused by a solar wind shock wave and/or cloud of magnetic field which interacts with the Earth's magnetic field.

Coronal Mass Ejection (CME)

A geomagnetic storm is due to a solar coronal mass ejection (CME) or a high-speed stream of the solar wind, containing magnetic particles, originating from a region of a weak magnetic field on the Sun's surface.

Geomagnetically Induced Currents (GIC)

Geomagnetically induced DC currents (GIC) can couple on to power lines and cause saturation in EHV transformers. In 1989, a geomagnetic storm energized ground induced currents which disrupted electric power distribution throughout most of the province of Quebec and caused aurorae as far south as Texas.

Second Order Harmonics (120Hz)

As a result of Extra High Voltage (EHV) transformers going into saturation they will produce second order harmonics that can damage Supervisory Control and Data Acquisition (SCADA) systems and related control equipment.

Electromagnetic Pulse (EMP)

An electromagnetic pulse, also sometimes called a *transient electromagnetic disturbance*, is an *electronic attack* using a short burst of electromagnetic energy and is generally disruptive or damaging to electronic equipment. The extent of interference or damage created by an EMP on electronic equipment is dependent on several factors: the power of the pulse, the dynamics of the pulse (rise time and frequency ranges), and the sensitivity of the target to the particular EMP. An E-Bomb capable of permanently knocking out the computers in an entire building has already been demonstrated. And, because of the increasing dependence on solid state integrated circuits and computer networks to control everything from backup generators to Building Automation Systems, such a device could also knock out HVAC systems, fire alarms, telephone systems, security cameras, security sensors and electronic locks. Basically, an E-Bomb would render a facility useless for command and control.

EMP

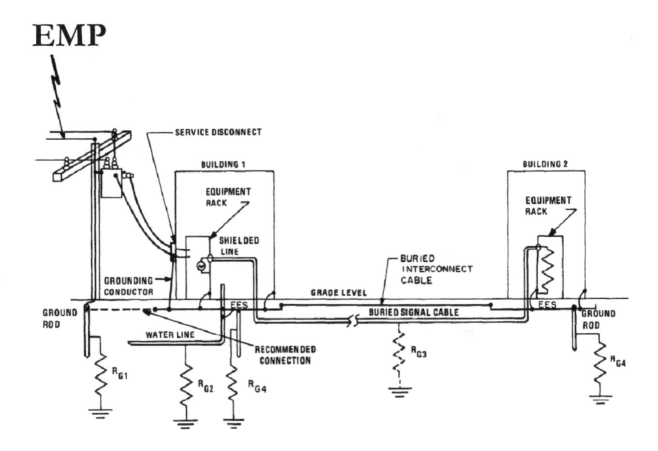

When military engineers talked about EMP, they were usually talking about Nuclear EMP (NEMP), High-Power Microwave (HPM) or High-Altitude EMP (HEMP). Nuclear EMP is a complex multi-pulse, usually described in terms of three components, as defined by the IEC, called "E1", "E2" and "E3". Although it seems counter-intuitive, thermonuclear weapons are less efficient at producing E1 and E2 EMP because the first stage can pre-ionize the air which becomes conductive and hence rapidly shorts out the Compton currents generated by the fusion stage. The E3 component of nuclear EMP is closely proportional to the total energy yield of the weapon. Hence, small pure fission weapons with thin cases are far more efficient at causing EMP than most megaton bombs and would be the weapon of choice by a determined adversary because they are cheaper and smaller.

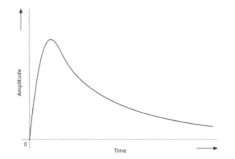

Most EMP pulses have a very sharp leading edge, building up quickly to their maximum level. The classic model is a double-exponential curve which climbs steeply, quickly reaches a peak and then decays more slowly.

E1 - The E1 pulse is the very fast component of nuclear EMP. E1 is a very brief but intense electromagnetic field that induces very high voltages in electrical conductors. E1 creates most of its damage by causing electrical breakdown voltages to be exceeded. E1 can destroy computers and communications equipment and it changes too quickly (nanoseconds) for ordinary surge protectors to provide effective protection against it, although there are special fast-acting surge protectors (such as those using TVS diodes) that will block the E1 pulse.

E2 - The E2 component is an "intermediate time" pulse that lasts from about 1 microsecond to 1 second after a nuclear explosion. E2 has many similarities to lightning, although lightning-induced E2 may be considerably larger than a nuclear E2. Because of the similarities and the widespread use of lightning protection technology, E2 is generally considered to be the easiest to protect against. The main problem with E2 is the fact that it immediately follows E1, which may have damaged the devices that would normally protect against E2.

E3 - The E3 component is very different from E1 and E2. E3 is a very slow pulse, lasting tens to hundreds of seconds. It is caused by the nuclear detonation's temporary distortion of the Earth's magnetic field. The E3 component has similarities to a geomagnetic storm caused by a solar flare. Like a geomagnetic storm, E3 can produce geomagnetically induced currents in long electrical conductors, damaging components such as power line transformers. Because of the similarity between solar-induced geomagnetic storms and nuclear E3, it has become common to refer to solar-induced geomagnetic storms as "Solar EMP." However, "Solar EMP" does not include an E1 or E2 component.

HPM is in the gigahertz-band frequencies (4 to 20 GHz) and HPM has the capability to penetrate not only radio front-ends, but also the most minute shielding penetrations throughout the equipment.

Effects of EMP

An energetic EMP can temporarily upset or permanently damage electronic equipment by generating high voltage and high current surges; semiconductor components are particularly at risk. The effects of damage can range from imperceptible to the eye, to devices being literally blown apart. Overhead utility power lines (even underground cables) will suffer damage. Cables, even if short, can act as antennas to transmit pulse energy to equipment. Solid state electronic equipment is susceptible to damage by large, but brief voltage and current surges. Equipment that is running at the time of an EMP is more vulnerable. Cars electronic circuits and cabling are likely too short to be affected and the metal frame provides some protection. During one nuclear test EMP disruptions were suffered aboard a KC-135 aircraft flying 190 mi from a 410 kt detonation. Small electronic devices, such as wristwatches and cell phones, would most likely withstand an EMP. The popular media often depict EMP effects incorrectly, causing misunderstandings among the public.

How Likely is an EMP Attack on a Data Center?

Granted, damage from an EMP attack on a data center is much less likely than a Geomagnetic Storm or a Coronal Mass Ejection, however in a recent SBIR RFP, the Defense Threat reduction Agency (DTRA) stated that EMP is an "imminent threat." An IEMI attack against a data center is much more likely. Unlike a cyber-attack where "fingerprints" can often be found for forensic analysis, an IEMI attacker will not leave any information behind. In fact, an IEMI shutdown of electronics is so rapid that the log files in the computers will not record the event.

Judging from open source statements and writings, many foreign analysts perceive a nuclear EMP attack as falling within the category of electronic warfare or information warfare, not nuclear warfare. In addition, some foreign analysts appear to regard EMP attack as a legitimate use of nuclear weapons. Recent technological advancements make use of a small non-nuclear EMP weapon (E-Bomb) much more likely. A determined enemy can use overt or clandestine EMP weapons against a military base as they can fit in a suitcase or fit in the back of a pickup truck. In fact, it is possible to purchase a 10-stage Marx generator built of ten 10nf per stage on the Internet that provides 1nf of erected capacitance. It has a maximum output of 160kV 13 Joule pulse of Rise time < 50 nanoseconds and is capable of shutting down computers at a distance of 15 meters.

An Iranian political-military journal, in an article entitled "Electronics to Determine Fate of Future Wars," suggests that the key to defeating the United States is EMP attack. China's most senior military theorist stated "… the country which possesses the critical weapons such as atomic bombs will have 'first strike' and 'second strike retaliation' capabilities. As soon as its computer networks come under attack and are destroyed, the country will slip into a state of paralysis and the lives of its people will ground to a halt Therefore, China should focus on measures to counter computer viruses, nuclear electromagnetic pulse…."

In addition, North Korean academic writings subscribe to the view that computers and advanced communications have inaugurated an "information age" during which the greatest strength, and greatest vulnerability, of societies will be their electronic infrastructures.

Nuclear EMP Weapons

An E-bomb is specifically designed to overwhelm electrical circuitry with a very intense electromagnetic field. A study conducted in the U.S. during the late 1980s reported that a high-yield device exploded about 500 kilometers above the ground can generate an EMP of the order of 50,000 volts over a radius of 2,500 kilometers around the point of burst which would be collected by any exposed conductor. Such an attack will not cause any blast or thermal effects on the ground below but it can produce a massive breakdown in the communications system. It is certain that most of the land communication networks and military command control links will be affected and it will undermine our capability to retaliate. Recently Russian and Chinese military scientists in open source writings describe the basic principles of nuclear weapons designed specifically to generate an enhanced-EMP effect, that they term "Super-EMP" weapons.

Non-Nuclear EMP Weapons

Non-nuclear electromagnetic pulse (NNEMP) is a weapon-generated electromagnetic pulse without use of nuclear technology. Unlike nuclear weapons which generate EMP as a secondary effect, the electromagnetic pulse from NNEMP weapons must come from within the weapon. This limits the range of NNEMP weapons but allows finer target discrimination. In a high-power microwave munition, the primary kill mechanism is the microwave energy, which greatly increases the radius and the footprint by, in some cases, several orders of magnitude. For example, a 2000-pound microwave munition will have a minimum radius of approximately 200 meters, or footprint of approximately 126,000 square meters. The effect of even small e-bombs would be sufficient for certain terrorist or military operations. Devices that can achieve this objective include a large low-inductance capacitor bank discharged into a single-loop antenna, a microwave generator, and an explosively pumped flux compression generator. To achieve the frequency characteristics of the pulse needed for optimal coupling into the target, wave-shaping circuits or microwave generators are added between the pulse source and the antenna.

Vircators are vacuum tubes that are particularly suitable for microwave conversion of high-energy pulses. NNEMP generators can be carried as a payload of bombs, cruise missiles (such as the CHAMP missile) and <u>drones</u>, with diminished mechanical, thermal and ionizing radiation effects, but without the political consequences of deploying nuclear weapons. Bofors HPM Blackout is a high-powered microwave weapon system, built by BAE Systems, which is stated to be able to destroy at distance a wide variety of commercial electronic equipment. The total weight of the weapon system is less than 500 kg. It is stated to be non-lethal to humans.

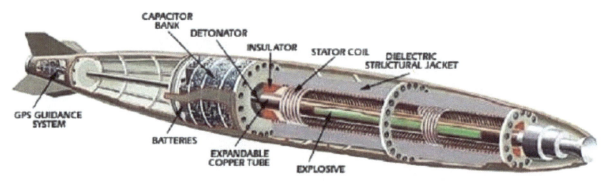

On March 25, 2003, CBS NEWS reported the first possible use of an e-bomb by noting that 'The U.S. Air Force has hit Iraqi TV with an experimental electro-magnetic pulse device called the "E-Bomb" in an attempt to knock it off the air and shut down Saddam Hussein's propaganda machine.

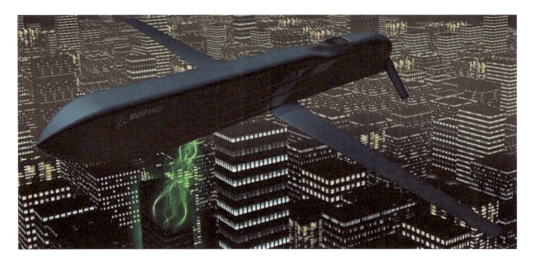

63

In a 2012 test, a Boeing CHAMP (Counter-Electronics High-Power Advanced Missile Project) missile successfully disabled the electronics in a two-story building by firing high power microwaves (a type of IEMI threat). Every PC inside went dark within seconds, as did the building's entire electrical system. The test was so successful that it also disabled cameras recording the event. Over the course of one hour, the missile knocked out electrical systems at seven selectively targeted buildings with little or no collateral damage. The weapon also demonstrated electromagnetic compatibility and hardening (to avoid a self-kill).

Electromagnetic weapons have evolved from experimental novelties destined for the battlefield to sophisticated threats capable of reaching behind the lines to neutralize the command, control and communications environment that's vital to national security. EMP weapons have become portable, affordable items that can be clandestinely deployed outside a building to damage all electronic circuitry including data centers and command headquarters, including the building support equipment such as, chillers, fire and smoke detectors, security systems and cameras, and back-up generators. They are readily available to anyone intent on causing major disruptions to any data center.

The next generation of electric vehicles such as the Tesla Model S and the Tesla Semi truck have a tremendous amount of energy that can be used to generate a very large non-nuclear EMP. They actually are raising the viability of a clandestine E-Bomb capable of neutralizing an entire building. Some of the 60 and 70 kWh versions of the Tesla Model S can even be "upgraded" to the 75 kWh version using software to unlock the extra capacity. Just like AT/FP criteria limit the proximity of parking setback from a DoD building, the setback for access of an electric vehicle to a data center should be restricted.

RF Weapon circa 2004

Suitcase RF Weapon circa 2016

Tesla Model S 75kWh Batteries

Mercedes Urban eTruck 1MW+

How Can We Harden Data Center Buildings and Energy Resources?

DoD requires that all components of an EMP-protected facility are designed to meet the requirements of MIL STD 188-125-1 and provide protection against the HEMP threat environment specified in MIL-STD-2169. Just as important as the electronic equipment in a mission-critical facility is the utility infrastructure that powers the facility. A microgrid can be designed to provide EMP-hardened electrical power generation and distribution capability sufficient to perform trans and post-attack missions, without reliance upon commercial electrical power sources.

A microgrid offers a way to connect on-base energy resources such as diesel generators, photovoltaic solar panels and battery storage so the military base can be "islanded" (disconnected from the civilian power grid) and continue to operate for an extended period of time. As of 2017, the DoD baseline requirement for stand-alone operation of mission critical buildings was raised from 72 hours to 14 days.

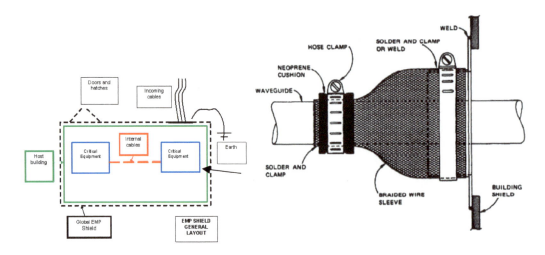

The first thing to consider is the construction of the data center building. There is a wealth of information available on the electromagnetic signal attenuation for the various construction materials used today.[3] The NIST report studied brick, masonry block, plain concrete, glass, lumber, drywall.

No matter what a building is made out of, we recommend a Faraday cage be constructed for mission critical spaces. Faraday's caging and metal encasing are considered to be the most effective protection against EMP. A Faraday Cage is a continuous conductive enclosure – an electromagnetic barrier - that meets or exceeds shielding effectiveness requirements and provides EMP-protected space within a facility. They are designed to divert and soak up the EMP and electrical surge protection circuits can provide additional protection. A Faraday cage works by three mechanisms: (1) the conductive layer reflects incoming fields, (2) the conductor absorbs incoming energy, and (3) the cage acts to create opposing fields. The conductive layer can be very thin because of something known as the "*skin effect.*" Layers of shielding separated by insulation works better than a single layer of thick metal sheeting. As a practical matter,

---

[3] NIST IR 6055, Electromagnetic Signal Attenuation in Construction Materials

wrapping with 2 or 3 layers of foil helps to assure that you actually have a good shield. Using heavy-duty aluminum foil can prevent the foil from tearing as easily.

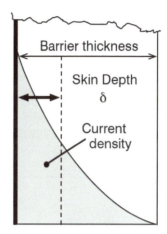

Material	Relative Conductivity (σ_r)	Relative Permeability (μ_r)	Skin Depth (δ)			
			50 Hz	10 kHz	1 MHz	100 MHz
Copper	1	1	9.3 mm	0.66 mm	66 µm	6.6 µm
Aluminium	0.6	1	12 mm	0.85 mm	85 µm	8.5 µm
Steel (ordinary cold-rolled)	0.16	200	1.5 mm	0.14 mm	100 µm	16 µm
Hi-perm. alloy(typ)	0.03	10 000	0.54 mm	54µm	*NA	*NA

(*) µr of Hi permeability alloys is generally collapsing above a few MHz.

Absorption losses (dB)

Thickness (mm)	Copper			Aluminium			Zinc			Steel			Copper Paint
	0.01	0.1	1	0.01	0.1	1	0.01	0.1	1	0.01	0.1	1	0.05
30 MHz	7	70	700	5.2	52	520	4	40	400	3	28	200	7
100 MHz	13	130	>1000	9.5	95	950	7	72	720	5	50	500	13
300 MHz	22	220	>1000	17	170	>1000	12	125	>1000	9	88	880	22

Examples of skin depth and absorption losses for some common metals

Most popular RFI shielding installed behind sheet rock is 16 Mesh Copper with a wire diameter of 0.0110 inches (0.2794 mm) and opening size 0.0510 inches (1.30 mm) and an opening area percentage of 67%. This is a plain weave with an overall thickness of 0.022 inches (0.5588 mm). I recommend a mill finish (uncoated). Magnetic shielding foil is available in high- and low-permeability versions to provide effective protection for sensitive electronic equipment exposed to electromagnetic interference and strong external magnetic fields. High-permeability foils work by absorbing external magnetic fields and redirecting them through the foil. Low-permeability foils are used for attenuating very strong, highflux external fields due to the foil's high saturation induction characteristics. Combining both high- and low-permeability foils to create one shield provides the widest range of magnetic shielding. The graph shows the direct current hysteresis loop for high-permeability foil with a thickness of 0.006in (0.152mm).

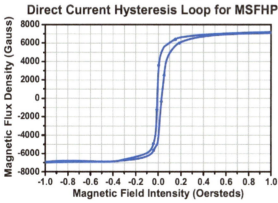

Unfortunately, most vital equipment needs to be in contact with the outside world. This contact point can allow the electromagnetic field to enter the cage thereby rendering any enclosure useless. There are ways to protect against these Faraday cage flaws, but the fact remains that this is a dangerous weak point.

We recommend a three-tiered design that provides *whole-building* shielding (Tier 1); *important room* shielding (Tier 2); and *critical equipment cabinet* shielding (Tier 3) for mission-critical equipment. Virtually all mission-critical communications-electronics and support equipment will be placed in the protected volume enclosed by the electromagnetic barrier and operate in a relatively benign electromagnetic environment, isolated from the external EMP stresses. No expensive EMP-unique performance characteristics would be required in design and selection of mission-critical systems (MCS) that will be housed within the protected volume. There would be no need to replace existing equipment with EMP-hardened versions.

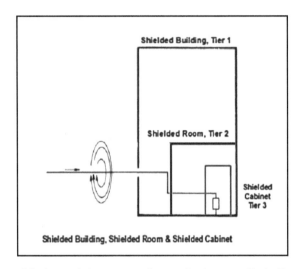

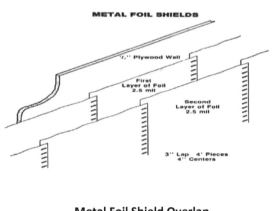

Metal Foil Shield Overlap

This low-risk approach results in a well-defined EMP protection subsystem configuration with inherent testability. The electromagnetic barrier consists of a EMP shield and Point-of-Entry (POE) treatments; it encloses the protected volume with three layers and prevents or limits EMP fields and conducted transients from affecting critical equipment. The electromagnetic barrier would include protected penetrations; more commonly, shielded cables or conduits and equipment cabinets and closed piping systems should be installed to provide the needed electromagnetic isolation from the protected volume. Electromagnetic closure is used to prevent excessive electromagnetic field leakage at an aperture POE. Examples of closure techniques at a seam between two metal plates include welding, brazing, or soldering and metal-to-metal contact under pressure applied with a mechanical fastening as shown below.

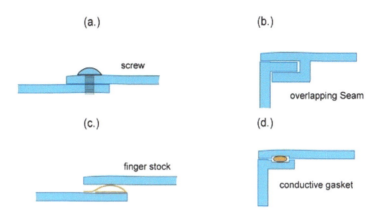

Care must be taken during the design of the data center to limit the number of electrical wires, cables or other conductive objects such as metal rods, that pass through the electromagnetic barrier to specially designed penetrating areas. These conductive POEs are also called *penetrating conductors*. Cables penetrating the exterior must be shielded or held to the same potential as the enclosure at all frequencies. A *penetration entry area* is that area of the electromagnetic barrier where long penetrating conductors (such as an electrical power feeder) and piping POEs are concentrated. The building design must ensure any intentional or inadvertent holes, cracks, openings, or other discontinuity in the EMP shield surface are eliminated. If it is necessary to provide holes in the shielded enclosure such as for equipment ventilation, it is better to have many small holes than a large hole. In the example below, the area represented by the small holes is equivalent to the area of the slots, but the small holes offer better protection. It is also possible to extend a hole into the building such as metal pipes or tubes which creates waveguides.

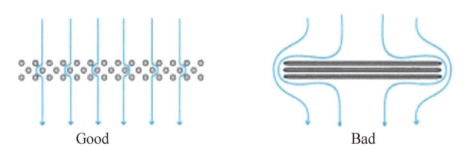

Intentional aperture POEs provided for personnel and equipment entry and egress and for fluid flow (ventilation and piped utilities) through the electromagnetic barrier must be carefully located to maintain the integrity of the electromagnetic barrier. EMP hardness is achieved through adhering to appropriate design specifications and should be verified by one or more test and analysis techniques.

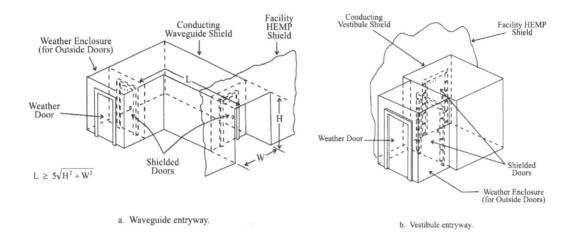

$L \geq 5\sqrt{H^2 + W^2}$

a. Waveguide entryway.

b. Vestibule entryway.

Thorlabs' 1-inch square conductive coated windows are available with one of three standard broadband antireflection coatings deposited on one surface, -A (350 - 700 nm), -B (650 - 1050 nm), or -C (1050 - 1620 nm), and a conductive Indium Tin Oxide (ITO) coating on the other surface. The coating thickness determines the balance between the sheet resistance of 50 - 80 Ω/sq. and optical performance. Contact to the conductive surface can be made by copper tape, a silver epoxy-painted busbar, a silver-loaded silicone gasket, or a conductive fabric over foam gasket. Never place wires directly in contact with the surface, or damage may result.

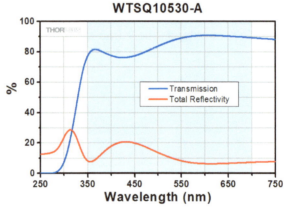

Conductive Window Transmission and Reflection

Data center utilities must be grounded using the equipotential ground plane method in accordance with guidance in MIL-HDBK-419. The EMP shield forms a major portion of the equipotential ground plane. Grounds for equipment and structures enclosed within the protected volume are electrically bonded to the inside surface of the shield. Grounds for equipment and structures outside the electromagnetic barrier are electrically bonded to the outside surface of the shield or to the earth electrode subsystem. Ground straps or cables used to connect the facility shield (equipotential ground plane) to the earth electrode subsystem are electrically bonded to the outside surface of the shield, and at least one such ground strap or cable shall be located at the penetration entry area. All grounding connections to the data center EMP shield must be made in a manner that does not create unprotected POEs.

A *hardness critical item* (HCI) is an item at any assembly level having performance requirements for the purpose of providing EMP protection. Nuclear HCIs provide protection from environments produced by a nuclear event or are specially designed to operate under nuclear weapon (device)-derived stresses. A *hardness critical assembly* is a top-level definable unit of EMP HCIs and other components, such as mounting hardware and terminal posts, that may not be hardness critical. A *hardness critical process* (HCP) is a process, specification, or procedure that is followed exactly to ensure that the associated HCI attains its required performance.

Norton equivalent circuit or Norton source is a circuit, consisting of a current source in parallel with an impedance, that has equivalent characteristics to those of the represented circuit over the operating range of interest. POE protective device or POE treatments are protective measures used to prevent or limit EMP energy from entering the protected volume at a POE. Common POE protective devices include waveguides below cutoff and electromagnetic closure plates for aperture POEs and filters and electric surge arresters on penetrating conductors. The three categories of electrical POE protective devices installed on penetrating conductors are *main barrier POE protective devices*, *primary special POE protective devices*, and *secondary special POE protective devices*. A main barrier electrical POE protective device is installed on an electrical conductor that penetrates from the system exterior, through the EMP shield, and into the protected volume. A Primary special electrical POE protective device is installed on an electrical conductor that penetrates from the system exterior, through the EMP shield, into a special protective volume. A primary special protective device is designed to provide the maximum attenuation possible without interfering with the normal operational electrical signals that are routed on the penetrating conductor. A secondary special electrical POE protective device is installed on an electrical conductor that penetrates from a special protective volume into the main protected volume. It is used only when necessary to augment the attenuation provided by the primary special POE protective device and the connected equipment.

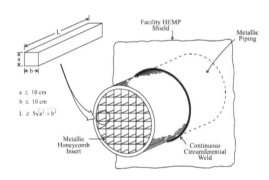

Typical waveguide-below-cutoff piping POE protective devices.

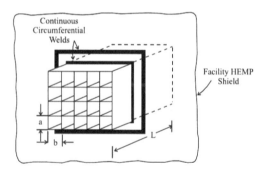

Typical waveguide-below-cutoff array ventilation POE protective device.

Special protective measures are hardening measures required in addition to implementation of the electromagnetic barrier. Special protective measures are necessary for MCS outside the barrier, for MCS that are within the protected volume and experience damage or upset during verification testing, and in cases requiring special protective volumes to provide supplementary isolation, when POE protective devices cannot satisfy the barrier requirements without interfering with facility operation. A waveguide below cutoff (WBC) is installed where required as a hardening measure. This is a metallic waveguide whose primary purpose is to attenuate electromagnetic waves at frequencies below the cutoff frequency (rather than propagating waves at frequencies above cutoff). The cutoff frequency is determined by the transverse dimensions and geometry of the waveguide and properties of the dielectric material in the waveguide. A waveguide-below-cutoff array is installed where required as a hardening measure. This an assembly of parallel waveguides below cutoff, with adjacent cells usually sharing common cell walls. A waveguide-below-cutoff array is used when the area of the shield aperture required to obtain adequate fluid flow within pressure drop limitations is larger than the permissible area of a single waveguide below cutoff.

Emprimus EMP.Alert™

The **Emprimus EMP.Alert™** is a detection solution that can provide an early warning for data and control center targets. It has the potential to detect a threat in time to take defensive action and, can help locate and eliminate it. The EMP.Alert™ can determine the cause of "unexplainable" outages, alert the users to potential data corruption from an attack and provide invaluable forensic information. It has a Frequency Response Range of MHz to 10+ GHz, a Pulse Rise Time <2 ns and E Field Amplitude data reports <100 V/m to100,000+ V/m.

EMP hardening measures should be integrated with design details of other disciplines, such as electromagnetic interference/electromagnetic compatibility, lightning protection, TEMPEST and with treatments for other hardening requirements such as Anti-Terrorism/Force Protection (AT/FP). The goal here is to provide an EMP-protected design based upon verifiable performance specifications.

MCS components outside the protected barrier, such as a radio antenna or evaporative heat exchanger, that must be placed outside the electromagnetic barrier, shall be provided with special protective measures as required to ensure EMP hardness. Breaker assembly comprised of two separate breakers will be installed. A DC disconnect breaker and an AC vacuum breaker. The DC breaker is designed to break DC and quasi-DC currents. The AC breaker has a high voltage stand-off that is opened second and protects the DC breaker. ABB Corp's **SolidGround**™ may be installed as needed. It automatically senses the presence of an EMP or induced harmonics, and blocks DC currents from flowing in the neutrals of large power transformers and triggering the protective mode with AC grounding through a low impedance capacitor bank. The system offers triple redundant fault protection when in the protective mode, providing spark gap voltage protection and breaker reclose if spark gap should fire.

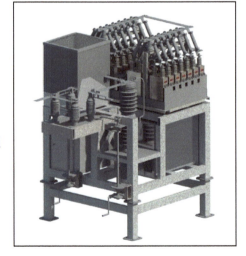

EMP Neutral Blocker

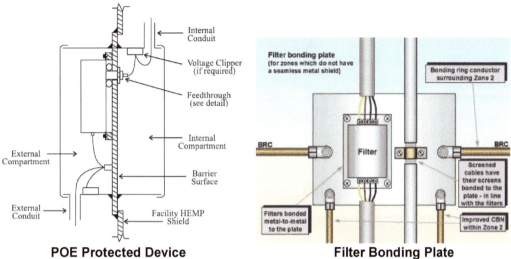

POE Protected Device **Filter Bonding Plate**

An EMP testing program that includes Pulsed Current Injection (PCI) Tests and Continuous Wave (CW) Immersion Tests will demonstrate that hardness performance requirements have been satisfied and that the required EMP hardness has been achieved. This program should include quality assurance testing during facility construction and equipment installation, acceptance testing for the electromagnetic barrier and special protective measures, and verification testing of the completed and operational facility. The data center designer should develop a 3D computer model of the facility. FEKO is a general-purpose 3D electromagnetic (EM) simulator that uses a computational electromagnetics software product developed by Altair Engineering. FEKO can compute electric and magnetic shielding factors for metallic or dielectric enclosures of arbitrary shape with arbitrary openings cut into them intended to shield internal cables or components from outside radiation. In this case, a plane wave is directed at the enclosure and field values computed inside the enclosure to test its effectiveness.

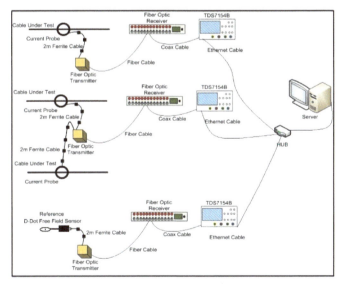

Data acquisition system.

A quality assurance program should be implemented during system construction and installation to demonstrate that the EMP protection subsystem materials and components comply with performance requirements of this standard. The quality assurance test procedures and results shall be documented and retained for use as baseline configuration and performance data. Acceptance of the EMP protection subsystem shall be based upon successful demonstrations of compliance with hardness performance requirements of MIL STD 188-125-1. EMP acceptance tests of the electromagnetic barrier and special protective measures should be conducted after all related construction work has been completed. Acceptance test procedures and results should be documented and retained for use as baseline configuration and performance data.

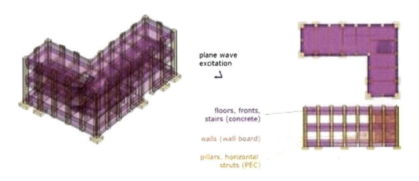

FEKO model of a two-story building analyzed with the EMP as an incident plane wave source.

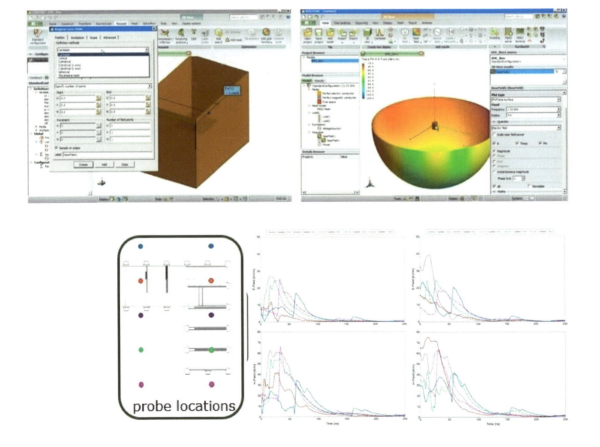

7. INSIDER THREAT

In 2011 Cybersecurity Watch Survey revealed that 60 percent of cyber-attacks come from outside entities. Sad to say, according to an IBM report, 55 percent of all attacks in 2014 were carried out by either malicious insiders or were inadvertent mistakes. A malicious insider with access to a data center BCS network has the potential to do the most physical damage to data center equipment and facilities. Insider threats to critical infrastructure are more serious than outsider threats because an outside attacker is less likely to know the BCS network vulnerabilities and its weaknesses as well as an insider would. I am primarily referring to building maintenance personnel here as I believe they are not as thoroughly vetted as data center IT personnel.

The primary insider threats are:
- Employees (and contractors) not following security protocols.
- Employee logging into an unsecured network, accidentally releasing a worm into the corporate network.
- Sloppy password administration (vendor default passwords not changed, ex-employee passwords not deleted and accounts not deactivated, passwords not changed regularly).
- Incorrectly installed systems that unintentionally bridge networks together.
- Improperly protected Human-Machine Interface (HMI).
- Unauthorized hardware/software on the network (key logger, wireless transmitter).

Insiders pose a cyber-threat because an employee could escalate access privileges in order to modify controls, turn equipment on/off, or drive equipment to failure. An insider can plant a worm or a Trojan horse in a BCS that can be activated quickly to cause multiple failures without further intervention. The insider could then *pretend to attempt to fix the problem*, meanwhile stepping around the true causes. The insider threat includes vendors who provide maintenance and support (typically via network or dial-in modem connections).

Types of Insider Threats

There are several categories of insiders and these can be further divided into those jobs that require employee have access to the BCS network, and those that do not. See Table below.

Insider Types	Descriptors
Insider (current or ex-employee)	Employee, contractor, vendor, utility company technician
Insider Associate	Has limited authorized access and escalates privileges.
Insider Affiliate	Insider by virtue of an affiliation, spoof the identity of the insider.
Outsider-Affiliate	Non-trusted outsider that uses an access point that was left open.

Insider Threat Types

Why would a data center employee want to damage the building equipment?

According to the FBI, these are the major reasons:
- Greed or Financial Need: A belief that money can fix anything. Excessive debt or overwhelming expenses.
- Anger/Revenge: Disgruntlement to the point of wanting to retaliate against the company.
- Problems at Work: A lack of recognition, poor performance rating, disagreements with co-workers or data center management, dissatisfaction with the job, a pending layoff, or passed over for promotion.
- Ideology/Identification: A desire to help the "underdog" or a particular cause.
- Divided Loyalty: Allegiance to another person or to a country besides the U.S.
- Adventure/Thrill: Want to add excitement to their life, intrigued by the clandestine activity, "James Bond Wannabe."
- Vulnerability to Blackmail: Extra-marital affairs, gambling, fraud.

What Type of Employee Behavior Would Indicate a Data Center Employee May be a Threat?

The behavioral characteristics of attackers are potential indicators and patterns to detect insider threat activity. The Figure below shows many types of observable employee behavior to look for which could serve as precursors to malicious activity. No one behavior by itself would be an issue, but questionable behaviors are more likely to be manifested in multiple observables.

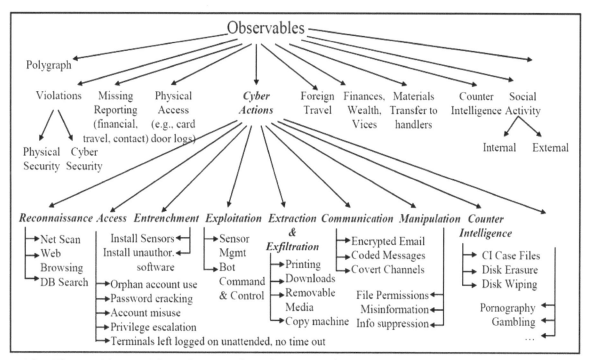

Insider Threat Observable Behaviors (Maybury 2006)

A great deal of research has been done concerning counterproductive work behavior in an effort to discover precursors by looking at personality predispositions. A study by Baron and Neuman suggests that organization changes (e.g., pay cuts, changes in management) frequently led to aggression. Robert Willison and Merrill Warkentin found *perceived injustice* as a common motivator for sabotage. A study by FEMA's Community Emergency Response Team's (CERT) Management and Education of Risks of Insider Threat (MERIT) project comparing IT sabotage and espionage identified personal predispositions and stressors as precursors of malicious events. Insiders historically telegraph their intent by exhibiting counterproductive work behavior.

Following are some examples:
- Not following security protocols.
- Log into unsecured network and release a worm into the corporate network.
- Sloppy password administration.
- Incorrectly install systems that bridge disparate networks together.
- Improperly protected Human-Machine Interface (HMI).

Most saboteurs share personal issues or predispositions that contribute to their risk of committing malicious acts. Some examples include:
- Stressful events, such as employer sanctions were precursors of sabotage and espionage.
- Concerning behaviors were observable before and during sabotage and espionage.
- Actions by technical insiders could have alerted the organization to planned or ongoing sabotage and espionage acts.
- Many organizations ignored or failed to detect rule violations.
- Lack of physical and electronic access controls facilitated IT sabotage and espionage.

Types of Insider Cyber-Attacks

An insider without complete access to the BCS network will perform reconnaissance on the BCS network where the devices are hosted to identify vulnerabilities. Common types of insider cyber-attacks include:
- SQL Injection – A code injection technique that exploits security vulnerabilities in an application, often targeting the backend database.
- Default Credentials – Attempt to log in to secure areas using default credentials.
- Dictionary Attack – A brute force attack against a HMI. HMIs with no lockout mechanisms can allow attackers to attempt multiple logins with little effort and no repercussions.
- Modbus Traffic Attack – Attempt to modify and execute valid commands issued by the HMI to the PLC (Modbus protocol sends traffic in clear text without requiring authentication).
- Denial or Disruption of Service – A denial of service attack could include shutting down routers, closing access to ports, deleting files, and renaming a server so other machines do not recognize it.
- Buffer Overflow – An overflow occurs when hacker sends more data than the buffer expects and nearby data gets overwritten.
- Spoofing – Spoofing exploits weaknesses in protocols to spoof users or reroute traffic. Spoofing servers allows hacker to gain unauthorized remote login and flood the network with garbage packets to knock a computer, sensor or control device off the network.

An insider can use Cain and Abel software which is a powerful multipurpose tool that can then sniff and crack passwords. The insider can also load a virus on a network like those shown in the Table below.

Boot Virus	Infects the boot sector of floppies or hard disks
Macro Virus	Written in Microsoft Office Macro language
Network Virus	Spreads via network shares
Stealth Virus	Hides in a file, copies itself out to deliver payload
Polymorphic Virus	Encrypts itself
Cavity Virus	Hides in the empty areas of executables
Tunneling Virus	Trace interceptor programs that monitor OS Kernel requests
Camouflage Virus	Disguise themselves as legitimate files

Computer Virus Types

It's important to note not all insider events are malicious, some, though well-meaning can be just as harmful. We know of an employee that downloaded a malicious worm that he thought was an anti-virus program.

8. 7x24

7×24 Exchange International is a not-for-profit organization that provides an educational forum focusing on challenges faced by mission critical industry professionals. Founded in 1989 by a group of industry visionaries, 7×24 Exchange International has grown to include over 375-member companies and 27 chapters. Members are as diverse as the industry itself and include firms within industries such as aerospace, energy, financial services, government, healthcare, pharmaceuticals, manufacturing, media, technology, and more. Through the expertise of its active membership, 7×24 Exchange International is a leading provider of conferences enabling collaboration and knowledge sharing amongst industry professionals. 7×24 Exchange International is committed to addressing the challenges of energy efficiency and sustainability, providing continued value to member companies and conference participants and giving back through its social responsibility initiative.

If you work in a data center and you are not a member, well, let's just say that you should be.

Go to: www.7x24exchange.org today.

Luis Ayala

Mr. Ayala began his career in 1970 when he was drafted during the Vietnam Police Action. With 40+ years experience, he has led federal construction programs for USACE, NAVFAC, GSA and the Intelligence Community. He is a former DoD Cyber Expert with in-depth experience on threat assessment, cyber attack vectors and deterrent planning. He is an avid writer on the subject of threats of cyber-physical attacks on America, and is a former Defense Intelligence Senior Leader at the Defense Intelligence Agency.

He is a Registered Architect, with an NCARB Certificate, is a LEED Accredited Professional and has a DAWIA Level III Certification. He received a Batchelor of Architecture Degree from Pratt Institute in New York, a Master of Administrative Science from the University of Alabama in Huntsville, and a Master of Science & Technology Intelligence from the National Intelligence University (NIU) in Washington DC. NIU is the only classified degree-granting institution in the United States. Lou's Masters Thesis at NIU is classified and the title is "Cyber-Secure Facilities for the Intelligence Community."

Lou is currently an independent consultant providing consulting services to a utlity company. Louayala16@gmail.com